CW00601495

Cast Away

screenplay and introduction written by
William Broyles, Jr.

preface to the script by
Robert Zemeckis

sp

First published 2001
by ScreenPress Books
28 Castle Street
Eye
Suffolk
IP23 7AW

Designed by Sarah Theodosiou
Printed in England by Cox & Wyman ltd., Reading, Berkshire

Design copyright © 2001 ScreenPress Books
All rights reserved
Compilation copyright © 2000 Newmarket Press
All rights reserved
Cover art, interior stills and text material © 2000 DreamWorks LLC and
Twentieth Century Fox Film Corporation
All rights reserved

William Broyles, Jr. is hereby identified as author of this work in
accordance with Section 77 of the copyright, Designs and Patents Act 1988

This book is sold subject to the condition that it shall not, be way of trade or otherwise,
be lent, resold, hired out, stored in a retrieval system, or otherwise circulated or
transmitted, in any form, or by any means, electronic, mechanical, photocopying,
recording or otherwise without the publisher's prior consent and without a similar
condition including this condition being imposed on the subsequent purchaser

A CIP record for this book is available from the British Library

ISBN 1 901680 57 6

For information on forthcoming ScreenPress titles please contact the publishers at:
– the address above
– fax: 01379 870267
– email: mail@screenpress.co.uk

or buy online at:
www.screenpress.co.uk

Contents

Zemeckis, Broyles, his wife Andrea, and Hanks on location near Amarillo, Texas.

Photo credit: Zade Rosenthal

Introduction by William Broyles, Jr.

Cast Away began in 1994 when Fox executive Elizabeth Gabler told me that Tom Hanks thought there might be a movie in the story of a modern man stranded on a desert island. The idea had immediate resonance for me. As a marine in Vietnam, I'd felt cast away from the world I'd known and then had to readjust when I returned. I'd worked at *Newsweek* and been obsessed with deadlines and time, not to mention *Time*. I'd re-read Robinson Crusoe not too long before, and been reminded what a powerful tale of isolation and resourcefulness it was.

At the time, Hanks was filming *Apollo 13*, a movie I co-wrote with Al Reinert, so I walked over and we discussed this island idea, which at the time he was jokingly calling *Chuck of the Jungle*. Sometimes the things Tom jokes about are the very things he takes most seriously. As we talked it became clear to both of us that this idea could be something interesting, we just didn't know what.

That first day Tom suggested that the main character might work for Federal Express. Sure, I thought, why not? I knew it was a good idea, but neither of us knew then just how good it was. FedEx turned out to be the perfect symbol of a modern company. Its business was connecting people around the world by eliminating the barriers of time and distance. It worked on deadlines every day, so it was dominated by the clock. Its trucks and packages were instantly recognizable around the world. Its motto, "The World on Time," conveyed an irony we could never manufacture.

Right away I could picture a FedEx truck at a deserted crossroads in Texas. I didn't know what it was doing there, but I knew that image would be in the movie. If we had tried to make up some bogus company, that image would never have worked. The audience would have been playing catch-up the whole movie. But using Federal Express jump-started everything. The audience could see that truck and know at once what it stood for.

But what was the story? For me it began with simple curiosity, rooted in E.M. Forster's classic admonition: "only connect." What if we took a man dedicated to making connections for a living and then disconnected that man from everything? What if we took a man anchored to the clock and set him adrift in a different sort of time? What would be left once we peeled off the soft layers of our modern life? What would be cast away? What would remain? What happens when your dreams don't come true? What's truly important in life?

Those questions could carry me as far and as deeply as I was capable of going. Wrestling with thematic elements – and others about acceptance and fate and forces larger than ourselves – was an important part of writing the screenplay, but those battles tend to play out at subconscious levels. They're hard to write about explicitly, and to do so in a movie would be as self-defeating as it would be presumptuous to write about them here.

So while these thematic questions were constantly at work beneath the surface, they weren't a story, and that's what a movie has to be. How that story was pieced together is the subject of this introduction. Instead of the profound questions, I had to ask myself simple ones. What do I do first? And then what do I do next? Those questions were, of course, eerily like the ones Chuck had to answer.

I began with that FedEx truck I kept seeing in my head. I decided to follow a real Federal Express package to see for myself what went into delivering it. Fred Smith, the chairman of FedEx, was a fellow marine, and we knew each other slightly from Vietnam veteran work. I asked him for his help but told him that he might never see the script, and that a FedEx plane would definitely have to crash. With those two conditions up front I didn't feel that FedEx would be helpful.

But Fred loves movies and he quickly gave his support, no strings attached. I immersed myself in Federal Express corporate culture. I interviewed dozens of FedEx employees and spent a night at the package sort in the Memphis super-hub, where thousands of workers sort millions of packages in the space of a few hours. The character of Chuck Noland began to take shape. He would be a trouble-shooter, a systems engineer, a FedEx true believer. Memphis was full of guys like that. When I described Chuck to Tom I could see that this sort of can-do character appealed to him. Chuck would be a sort of cousin to Jim

Lovell, the astronaut Tom played in *Apollo 13* who was set adrift in space and had to improvise his way home.

By fits and starts I came up with a basic outline for the story: set up Chuck's very modern life, take everything in that life away and see how he survives, then return him to a world that has gone on without him. It was in a way the classic mythic journey of departure, adventure, return. It seemed to have the potential to accomplish what Tom and I wanted. We talked, I wrote, we talked some more. And the script began to take shape.

It would begin with the image of that FedEx truck on the plains of my home state of Texas, what would appear visually to be the middle of nowhere. It would use geography, the vastness of the plains and the ocean, as a character. A FedEx box would play a central role, a box marked with something special. When my wife Andrea, an artist, gave me a monoprint of two angel wings, I knew that was what would be on the box, and that the box would end up being Chuck's guardian angel. I just didn't quite know how.

I then went on to write a first rough draft that contained many of the basic elements that would end up years later in the movie. Tom and I were encouraged by it, but we both knew the script was a long way from being done. The most immediate problem was that the scenes on the island – the very heart of the movie – felt inauthentic, like a hash of *Gilligan* re-runs and my research into castaway narratives and primitive man.

So I went down to the Sea of Cortez with some experts in primitive technology and tried to survive as Chuck would have. I had to make shelter and find something to drink and eat. I struggled to open a coconut, failed miserably to spear a fish, and ended up trying to eat a crab raw. The raw crab led me to the epic of making fire, which, believe me, is far harder even than it looks on film.

But once I had managed to survive physically, I realized that I faced an entirely new challenge: loneliness. After an interminable night watching the stars circle I went down to the beach. There on the sand was a volleyball, washed up by the tide. Eventually I decorated it with shells and seaweed and began calling it by its brand name. I had learned for myself what I knew already, that man is a social animal. We aren't meant to be alone. And now I had a companion: Wilson.

Virtually all of this experience passed into the screenplay, including Wilson. The time I spent on the Sea of Cortez gave me a strong realistic basis for the island sequence. It also convinced both Tom and me that Chuck would have to make a dramatic journey from physical to spiritual and emotional survival. That's when I started thinking of a time cut that would bring down the curtain on Chuck's physical challenges and prepare us for the next stage of his journey. I decided that the time cut would come when, as a consequence of not having the medical care we take for granted, Chuck would have to do something I could not imagine doing: knock out his own tooth. The thought of that made my mind go blank. I decided the screen might as well too.

I had the material; the next question was how to write these island scenes, a great portion of the movie, without dialogue to help carry them on. Chuck was re-creating the journey of humanity, from the making of stone tools and the discovery of fire through the creation of art. Stripped of everything that made him modern, he would have to find in himself the primitive core of mankind. Likewise, in writing the movie I had to strip away dialogue and return to the core of film: action. Everything Chuck did had to be logical, dramatic, and entertaining. It had to be real, not convenient or cute. Anything remotely reminiscent of *Swiss Family Robinson* or *Gilligan's Island* Tom would ax immediately. I began calling him the Gilligan's cop.

Even people in the movie business assume that a screen writer only writes dialogue. And certainly some of the dialogue scenes were hard to write, particularly the scenes at the end between Tom and Helen Hunt. But the challenge in the island section reminded me of the old saying that you don't miss your water till the well runs dry. We depend so much on words to carry our stories, on so-called dramatic conflict between our characters. But I had no other characters, only Tom and the island. But there was drama. And there was action.

The key was conveying the drama and the action so that the audience would understand what was going on in Chuck's head. In the early versions I had him talking to himself at key places, even though I knew I would eventually cut those lines out. It was the best way to remind myself of what he was thinking and why one scene should follow another. For the same reason, whenever Chuck talked to Wilson I gave Bob and Tom some notes of Wilson's side of the conversation, so Tom would know what he was responding to.

I tried to organize the first sections based on what Chuck knew, and not to jump ahead. At first he would wait to be rescued. Then he would explore his surroundings and discover he was on an island, a moment of discovery I decided to connect to discovering the pilot's body, so that isolation and mortality would be indelibly linked. When the chance came he would have to try to escape, an attempt I determined to make so daunting we would believe it was impossible. When escape ended in disaster he would realize he was truly stranded and then devote himself full-time to survival. Then and only then would he open the FedEx packages he had sorted and prepared for delivery. That's just the kind of guy he is.

From the beginning we decided not to impose a superior narrative structure on Chuck's struggle. There would be no voice-over to explain what was happening, no cuts back to Memphis and the anxiety of the rescue attempts. There would be just the hard challenges of survival and Chuck's response to them, his halting, improvised mastery of his environment. At its core the drama would be physical. Chuck's own body would be the canvas of the action. It would start out soft and pale and awkward; it would be bruised, cut, scraped, punctured; and it would emerge four years later tanned and hard, with all the fat burned away and the reality of what he had endured written in his eyes.

That's a tall order, and it puts a huge burden on the actor. But having Tom Hanks in mind from the beginning meant I could visualize an actor who could convey his thoughts and feelings without words, who had the transparent intelligence that would let us see him connect the dots. But that wasn't all. Tom's body had to change dramatically, so that the first time we saw Chuck after four years we would know instantly what he had gone through. The experience was literally wasting him away. We shot the first half of the movie and then broke for a year so Tom could lose more than fifty pounds. There were times when Bob Zemeckis and I wouldn't hear from Tom for a few weeks. We had nightmares about him hiding out at McDonald's wolfing down Big Macs with fries.

When Tom showed up with the weight gone we were stunned at how different he looked. We knew then and there that the movie could work. It was the most concrete physical example of what lengths Tom went to for this movie. Another thing about Tom: he could have had this script filmed any time he wanted to, but he felt, and I hoped, that there was something special in this story, and that we could find it if we did not allow ourselves to be too easily satisfied. We threw out our first ideas, then our tenth ideas, too, and our twentieth, then came back and resurrected early ideas but in slightly different form, changed just enough finally to serve the story.

But I'm jumping ahead. When Bob finally came on board for good the process of working on the script changed. Instead of my working with Tom, I worked with Bob, then Tom would come in and we would all talk over where we were. It was a collaboration in spirit and in fact. Each of us took turns lifting the others out of those moments when we felt we'd never figure it out, and from those even darker moments when we would look at each other and wonder if anyone would really be interested in this movie, if in fact we weren't out of our minds.

In our story, Chuck is forced to pare away everything in his life, all the conveniences, all the connections we assume are ours by right. I did the same in writing the script itself, kept burning off the fat, tightening it up. At one point it was 125 pages. The shooting script was 92. Bob accelerated that process. He knew what could and should be filmed and what didn't have to be. "That'll never be in the movie," he would say, and I knew that was one more bit or even whole scene that could be cut. Then I'd try something new and he might say, "That'll work," or, "Well, anybody can do that," meaning: it was too predictable, try again, dig deeper.

As for the island sequences, it was Bob's visual genius that ultimately made them work, that and his confidence (not always either unflagging or shared; see below) that the audience would find them as fascinating as he did. For years I had imagined the island a certain way, free from the realities of having to film it. When Bob and I went location hunting, we were shown a remarkable uninhabited island in Fiji called Monu-riki. It was the perfect antagonist for Tom, the most important piece of casting after him and Helen Hunt.

The script would now enter a new phase: it would have to reflect the actual location and express what could and should actually be filmed. Tom's movements over it would have to be tracked exactly.

And the island spurred some new ideas. For example, there was a broken tree on the summit that offered dramatic possibilities, a cave high on a rock wall that could be Chuck's shelter, and a large rock which could be the headstone for the pilot's grave.

One part of the script kept nagging at Bob, and at Tom, too. Originally I had Chuck saved by Japanese scuba divers who wandered onto his island. It was a relic of when the script indulged in a certain broad humor. Bob was convinced that Chuck couldn't be rescued that way. "Can't we do something else?" he kept asking me. When I suggested Chuck could risk his life and try to escape, that's when Bob committed completely to the movie.

Every scene I wrote was made better by how Bob imagined it, by how he challenged me to make it better, by his passion for the power of detail. Since we had little dialogue, physical detail became crucial. Just coming up with the pocket watch with Kelly's picture, a single prop that combined Time and Love and that would keep Helen Hunt's character present on the island, was worth a dozen pages of great talk.

I never thought I could devote so much writing time to what happened to every piece of Chuck's wardrobe, or how to imagine the most unexpected thing inside each FedEx box and then come up with what Chuck would do with it. The few words I could have him say I would have to write, for example, on the birthday card inside the box containing Wilson. But it was worth it: the inanimate characters – the island, the watch with Helen's picture, Wilson the volleyball, the Angel Wings box, the PortaPotty, the ice skates, the raft – virtually steal the movie.

Once I had the idea of Chuck's escape from the island, I had the opportunity to do a section where he would be rescued at sea just as he had been lost at sea years before. The escape would be inspired ultimately by the wings on the FedEx box, those wings that I had always suspected would play a major role but just what that role would be for years I didn't know. Chuck would paint them on his sail, and when the sail finally blew away he would say, not "it's gone," but "they're gone." The ocean sequence led to the whale, the loss of Wilson, and the letting go of the oars, episodes that work as adventure or as deeply as anyone would care to take them.

So much of writing this script was like an actor doing different takes or a musician practicing different approaches to a concert, with Bob and Tom there to help me figure out what was working and what wasn't. On one draft I would focus on the love story, on another I would experiment with layering in Chuck's life in Memphis. For example, I gave Chuck a family and an office and a secretary. I had him play softball and do charity work. I cut it early on. I wrote and we filmed an extended credit sequence that followed the first Angel Wing box from Texas through Memphis to Russia. After the first test screening we cut everything except the beginning and the end. We filmed a few other scenes of Chuck's office life in Memphis. They weren't necessary. The audience got who Chuck was right away.

To mark the depths of Chuck's despair on the island I originally had him try to commit suicide and fail. Then Bob happened to watch a particularly embarrassing attempted suicide in another movie. "Look what we almost did," Tom said. I took the whole sequence out and left it a shared experience between Chuck and Wilson, a point of contention that Wilson kept bringing up to Chuck's increasing irritation, the impetus for his flinging Wilson away.

The suicide attempt was treated dramatically like making the raft. We withheld what really happened. We don't learn until later that Chuck wanted to use the PortaPotty for a sail. We don't learn the full story of what happened with that rope and the broken tree until the very end. Like having no dialogue or not opening the Angel Wing box or the ending itself, this strategy of withholding information was intended to increase the audience's involvement in the story.

When Chuck was rescued I originally devoted pages of the script to show his re-entry into modern society. I had him treated in a hospital. I experimented with giving him his job back. I gave him an apartment, had him spar with the media, become an artist. For a long time he rode a bicycle everywhere. I showed him buying a new Wilson and figuring out where to return the Angel Wings package. All that I cut. There was no time for it.

Besides, everything in those scenes was told completely by having Chuck sleep on the floor and click a fire-starter off and on, and by placing a new volleyball and the Angel Wings package on the seat of his car. That was a central lesson for me: trust the power of visual information. In almost every case, the audience doesn't need words to understand. It doesn't need things explained. It can see them.

One unexpected problem was that the loss of Wilson was so wrenching that it gave me a particularly difficult challenge: how to make Chuck's ultimate loss of Kelly as emotionally powerful as his loss of a volleyball. I tried everything. I had her visit him at a hospital in Hawaii, I had him show up unexpected on her porch, I had them go off together. But nothing worked. Whenever I fell back on traditional dramatic conflict, the scene just died.

Finally I just tried having Chuck and Kelly come together knowing that they would always love each other but also knowing there was nothing they could do about it. I set the goal of having them not talk about what happened, having everything beneath the surface, until the very last possible moment. It became her scene almost more than his. He's now found, she's now lost.

After being so determined to challenge the audience the whole movie, after putting all our faith in its ability to understand what Chuck was going through, we ultimately decided we needed one moment where we got inside Chuck's head. We needed one moment where he would tell us what had happened and how he felt. That led to the scene after he lets Kelly go, when he tells his friend Stan about his suicide attempt and why he decided to stay alive no matter what, even when he had no hope.

That bridge scene was the very last one I wrote. I wanted to tie Chuck's past experience on the island to his unknown future, and give resonance to what had gone before and what was to come. With all my dedication to the power of visual drama, I would love to have done the movie without it. But sometimes there are emotions and truths only words can convey.

Writing the very ending was a struggle. I wish like Mozart I could see everything perfectly in my head and just write it down. But I have to write to find out what I think. For a time I even gave Chuck a new life, with a new wife and children. They fell in love after he opened the Angel Wing box he had spent four years returning to her. But that was too specific. It diminished what he went through. So I sealed up the Angel Wing box. I omitted Chuck's future. Instead I left him at the crossroads we saw in the very beginning, with his whole life ahead of him. He delivers the Angel Wing box, but really it delivers him. Even the middle of nowhere is somewhere.

It's a cliché to say a movie is a collaboration. But no one films the pages of a script. They have to be brought to life. Every writer should be so lucky as to work with talented people like Tom Hanks and Bob Zemeckis who can make the simplest bit of writing soar. It may be my script, but it's their movie. We worked together on it from beginning to end. We disagreed, we were stumped, we found solutions, together. For all the changes I took the script through over those six years, it is still, thanks to them, absolutely true to what I had first wanted it to be.

As *Cast Away* seems to be finding some commercial success, it's important to point out that by making essentially a silent movie without the usual satisfying Hollywood ending we were taking a huge gamble. As usual, Tom said it best. "The audience'll either love it, or they'll walk out of the movie wondering, 'What were those guys thinking?'" While we were working on it we were acutely aware we might be shipwrecking ourselves. At those moments Bob would say something like, "But if we don't make a movie like this, who will?" And, in the end, when it was all done, we had that rare pleasure – certainly rare for the writer – of knowing that even if it failed commercially we had made the movie we wanted to make. Even if Chuck spoke to no one else, he spoke to us.

We shot the last scene of the movie on the last day of principal photography. Bob and Tom and I were all there, our six-year journey with the script and Chuck's four-year journey both coming to a kind of end. There was Chuck, there was his jeep, his new Wilson, the beat-up FedEx Angel Wing box. And there were the four roads I had imagined many years ago, stretching away, across plains as featureless as the ocean surrounding Chuck's island. He could take one road, he could take another. It almost doesn't matter which one. His suffering and his loss have freed him. His future is ahead of him. As I wrote in the script, the end is the beginning.

Acknowledgements

Many people worked incredibly hard to bring this script to life. Dave Wescot and David Holladay of the Boulder Outdoor Survival School and Steve Watts of the Schiele Museum of Natural History were my guides back to our primitive past. Among the cast, Helen Hunt as always was extraordinary; Nick Searcy, Chris Noth, and Lari White brought intelligence and empathy to their scenes. The crew on this movie was amazingly dedicated. Many of them I knew only by their work, which was extraordinary. Others inspired me by their passion for this project.

Rick Carter, Artie Schmidt, Don Burgess, and Alan Silvestri transformed words into art. Steve Starkey, Jack Rapke, Joan Bradshaw, Cherylanne Martin, and Josh McLaglen sweated out every detail on both sides of the camera. Tom Jacobson helped launch us and Tom Rothman kept the bar high. Sheila Gallien read every single draft and kept my writing honest. Bob Bookman, Tory Metzger, Tom Hansen, Tom McGuire and David Barndollar kept me going. Elizabeth Gabler believed in this from the beginning to the end.

My wife Andrea and her art inspired me, just as it did Chuck. She and my children David, Susannah, Katie and James were marooned with me for years as I worked on this script. They all helped me more than they will ever know. I'm sure they are as glad as I am to be rescued at last.

Chuck's first word of dialogue in the movie is "time." Time runs his life and for six years time ran our lives as we made this movie. His last words are "thank you," an expression of gratitude which defines his transformation. And those are my last words as well. To all the people who worked so hard on *Cast Away*, thank you.

Preface to the Script by Robert Zemeckis

Five years ago Bill Broyles showed me a script he and Tom Hanks jokingly called *Chuck of the Jungle*. At the time I was about to make *Contact*, but Bill's script stayed with me. It wasn't just because it was well written, which it was, even though it was also clearly a work in progress. It was that I couldn't pigeonhole it. It was an adventure story, a love story, a fable. It had the potential to work at all kinds of levels, just as I hope *Forrest Gump* and *Contact* do.

A year later they showed an improved version. It was called *Cast Away* now. This time it glowed. I had no choice. I simply had to do it. There was too much wonderful stuff in there, too many opportunities, too many challenges. Some scripts you read and you can see how to do them right away. *Cast Away* wasn't like that. I didn't know how to do it, and that meant I had to.

So while Tom went off to make *The Green Mile*, Bill and I put our heads together on the script. At the time Bill had Chuck rescued by Japanese scuba divers. It seemed too deus ex machina, too convenient. So Bill came up with the breakthrough idea of having Chuck escape from the island. He would have to choose whether to stay there or risk his life to get off. That clinched it for me. I knew we had our movie.

Of course that solution created its own challenge: how would he escape, anyway? The tide would have to bring him something. Bill came up with barrels that would float him over the reef, but that didn't seem cinematic enough. Then we thought up a sail, something that would power him over the waves. The form that sail took was one of those mysterious moments of creativity, like having Chuck paint Wilson's face with his own blood, that simply can't be explained. If you work hard enough and dig deeply enough, sometimes they just happen.

Once we had the escape sequence Bill came up with this image of Chuck letting go of the oars. Chuck had tried everything, he had done

Zemeckis and Hanks rehearse scenes in Moscow.

all he could. There was nothing left but to give himself up to the ocean, to fate, to God. And that's when, after all his efforts, he would be rescued. That to me was one of the central themes of the movie: acceptance. Life isn't a problem to be solved, but a mystery to be lived. That sense of mystery is there in Bill's script, and I hope it's on the screen.

In filming Bill's script I came up with different camera approaches for each section. The opening scenes are all shot with Steadi-cam or hand-held to create the sense of constant movement that is Chuck's life. Once he is on the island, time changes and so does how he experiences it. I locked the camera down and moved it only on two axes so we would have to slow down just as Chuck did. I decided to have no score on the island, nothing to mitigate his isolation for the audience. We hear only what Chuck hears: the wind, the surf, thunder and rain, the creaking of the palm trees. Once he gets back, the camera is more active, circling around him, positioning him for his new life.

The island sequences were some of the most complex filming of my career. The action had to be logical, it had to be entertaining, it had to be dramatic. Luckily I had Tom Hanks, whose acting brilliance is, among other things, to let us see how his mind works without telling us. Tom put himself on the line. He made everything simple and honest and therefore good.

But it all came from the script, from having every beat thought out backwards and forwards, down to the details of what happened to every piece of Chuck's clothing and how Chuck makes use of what's inside those FedEx boxes. And it came from Bill researching Chuck's ordeal himself and coming up with inventive approaches to the challenges of survival, from opening a coconut to building a fire.

We liked filming without dialogue so much we carried it over into the rest of the movie. One of my favorite scenes Bill wrote is when Tom comes back from Russia. The typical scene would have had Chuck and Helen Hunt exchanging banalities or blathering on with exposition about their relationship. Bill wrote it where Tom stares at her for a long Frank Capra moment and then, instead of talking, they dance to the sound of the Xerox machine. That felt real to me, the way couples really act.

It was the standard we tried to meet on all the scenes between the

Zemeckis and Hanks rehearse a scene in Fiji.

two of them. Even at the most crucial moment when Chuck's returned, where you don't know which way the scene is going, they talk about the Super Bowl. That moment does so much. It tells us Chuck's missed a lot, it re-establishes their intimacy, and, by the example of losing by "one lousy yard," it reinforces the deeper theme of chance and loss.

Finally we had to figure out how to end the movie, of how to sum up what all this had meant to Chuck. Bill tried any number of specific scenes, all of them perfectly fine. But he felt, and I agreed, that the more specific we became the more we diminished what Chuck had been through. Bill had always had this image of a Texas crossroads. It was the perfect symbol for what had happened to Chuck. His new life was beginning. He could go in any direction and be okay.

Bill likes to say we did the movie the way Chuck survived: by trial and error, by testing one solution, failing, trying another. That was certainly Bill's path on the script. Sometimes the problems seemed insoluble. But there's a lot of Chuck in Bill. He never gave up.

We worked together every step of the way, from pre-production right down to the last changes we were making a week before the premiere. Most of them involved cutting. For example, Bill wrote and we filmed several scenes about Chuck's FedEx life. But it was clear the audience got who he was right away. We didn't need to tell them over and over. And that is one of the strengths of Bill's script. It trusts and challenges the audience. It certainly challenged me.

I am as proud of this movie as anything I have ever filmed. I'm grateful Bill and Tom turned the oars over to me. I hope they're as proud of the result as I am.

Cast Away

FADE IN:

EXT. PANHANDLE OF TEXAS DAY WIDE
We open on the Texas plains, horizon to horizon, nothing but brown earth and blue sky. The blank slate of nature, the absence of man. A plume of dust comes into frame. The dust is from a TRUCK with "Federal Express" blazoned across the side. It crosses a four-cornered intersection and heads down another road.

EXT. RANCH HOUSE MOMENTS LATER
The truck turns into a ranch yard with a neat house in front and a large barn behind it, passing an artistic-looking mailbox with "Dick and Bettina Peterson" written above it in weathered iron. Around the barn are large sculptures, some of angel wings that turn gently in the wind.

EXT. BARN/STUDIO SAME
The DRIVER (RAMON) gets out of the truck and heads for the barn. In the b.g. we see a woman welding at her work space. Next to the door is a table with a coffee-maker, a steaming cup of coffee, and a FedEx box ready for pickup.

                         RAMON
     Is this it, Mrs. Peterson?

She lifts up her welding mask, but we still don't see her face.

                         WOMAN
     That's it.
(beat)
     I'll have another one Tuesday.

He admires a drawing of TWO ANGEL WINGS united by a set of loosely drawn rings.

                              RAMON

        Nice. Where's it headed?

                              WOMAN

        She's snowbound, Ramon.
(beat)

        Oh, your coffee's right there!

                              RAMON

        Got it! Thanks.

He tucks the box under his arm, picks up the coffee, and heads for
the truck.
We stay with the package as he sets it down inside the truck. Doors
close. Ka-chunk!

CREDITS BEGIN

INT. FEDEX OFFICE AMARILLO, TEXAS DAY
Doors open. We're with the package as hands take it from the truck,
thrust it into a container, then roll the container through the open
doors of a big Semi. Doors close.

CREDITS CONTINUE

EXT./INT. FEDEX SUPERHUB MEMPHIS NIGHT
Doors open. We're assaulted by the bizarre late-night world of the
MEMPHIS FEDEX SUPERHUB. From the plane, we race across the tarmac,
on a dizzying ride with a million other packages. Mechanical arms
bang the package from belts to chutes to belts again, then into
another container. Doors close.
The scene is black for a long time.

INT. RUSSIA CUSTOMS SHED NIGHT
Boom! We're dumped out of a sack onto a conveyor belt in a room
covered with signs in Russian. In front of us is a TUBE PACKAGE with
FRAGILE signs all over it. RUSSIAN WOMEN in customs uniforms are
stamping packages on the belt ahead of us. Bam! They take extra care

in stamping the Fragile Box very hard. Bam! The Angel Wing Box is stamped! Then whoosh! It's dropped off the belt, down a twisting chute.

Suddenly it's black again.

INT. FEDEX OFFICE MOSCOW DAY

Raucous Russian voices, the clink of glass on glass. A container opens. The Fragile Box is next to us. Surrounding the container are Federal Express employees smoking cigarettes and drinking vodka and not looking all that interested in delivering packages. The driver closest to us, FYODOR DOLOKHOV, pours one last glass, then sticks the vodka bottle into the container. The doors close.

CREDITS CONTINUE

INT. FEDEX OFFICE MOSCOW NIGHT

It's quiet except for a woman's giggling. The doors open again and Fyodor takes out the vodka bottle. He pours a drink for a RUSSIAN WOMAN, then puts the bottle back. It's dark again.

INT. FEDEX OFFICE MOSCOW NIGHT HOUR LATER

We hear the sounds of raucous sex. Suddenly a foot KICKS OPEN the door! We see naked female legs spread-eagled. Between them is Fyodor, his back to us. In the throes of passion the woman KICKS the door shut! Black again.

CREDITS END

INT. FEDEX OFFICE MOSCOW DAY

We hear urgent voices in Russian, sounds of scuffling, bottles being emptied into a trash can. The doors open. Fyodor reaches in and grabs packages as YURI ROSTOV, the supervisor, buttons his shirt over a gold necklace and yells in Russian, "Hurry! Hurry!"

There's a flurry of activity: floors being swept, packages stacked, trash cans emptied of vodka bottles. In the b.g. we see a LADDER being brought in.

EXT. MOSCOW STREETS DAY

The door opens on a winter scene. Snow. Slush. A few Christmas lights adorn a residential building. Fyodor takes the Angel Wing Box out and walks toward it.

EXT. MOSCOW APARTMENT DAY MOMENTS LATER

A young American man, DICK PETERSON, signs the form and takes the Angel Wing Box. A BEAUTIFUL RUSSIAN WOMAN puts her arms around the man. We hear in accented English, "It's pretty. Who is it from?" "My wife," Dick replies.

The package goes inside. We don't. We stay with Fyodor as he ambles back toward the truck. Several letters are missing from the truck's logo, so the side of the truck reads only ED X.

EXT. MOSCOW RESTAURANT DAY MOMENTS LATER

Fyodor has just delivered the Fragile Box to an OLD WOMAN in a neighborhood restaurant filled with Russians hunched over borscht and black bread. The old woman yells over the din.

OLD WOMAN

Nicolai!

NICOLAI, a young boy, runs in. The Old Woman gives him the package and takes out a card, checks the address and gives the boy directions. "Go! Go!" She exhorts the boy in Russian as he heads out the door.

EXT. MOSCOW STREETS MOMENTS LATER

Nicolai carries the Fragile Box through the streets of Moscow, into Red Square, dodging traffic, splashing through slush and snow.

EXT. MOSCOW DAY MOMENTS LATER

Nicolai runs by a huge statue of Lenin.

EXT. MOSCOW DAY MOMENTS LATER

Nicolai runs across the Moscow River.

EXT. FEDEX OFFICES MOSCOW DAY

Nicolai runs in the door.

INT. FEDEX OFFICES MOSCOW DAY

A lone SECURITY GUARD lounges by the entrance, next to a panelled wall. Nicolai runs by the Security Guard as we hear, over:

> CHUCK (O.S.)
> Time. We live by it, ladies and gentlemen, but it doesn't live by us. Time doesn't care if we're male or female, black or white, American or Russian...

Nicolai takes us toward the voice, which seems to be coming from a group of RUSSIAN FEDERAL EXPRESS EXECUTIVES who are standing around the base of the ladder we had seen being carried in. Among them we find Yuri, the supervisor, who carries a clipboard, symbol of his authority. As Chuck talks, Yuri translates.

We follow their gazes up the ladder to where a FedEx troubleshooter named CHUCK NOLAND, mid-thirties, installs a digital clock. He fixes the final details using a screwdriver on a Swiss Army knife attached to a keychain.

> CHUCK (cont'd)
> ... it doesn't care if you pray to Buddha or dance around a fire.

Yuri exchanges can-you-believe-this glances with his colleagues.

> CHUCK (cont'd)
> That's why every FedEx office has a clock, a clock just like this one. Because we live or we die by the clock. Because we can never commit the sin of turning our back on time!

Chuck sets the countdown portion of the digital clock with a remote device. It reads 03:07:00.

> CHUCK (cont'd)
> Three hours, seven minutes until the end of today's package

sort. That's all the time we've got! We either beat that clock or –

Chuck catches a glimpse of Nicolai on the edge of the crowd.

>   CHUCK (cont'd)
> Nicolai! Excellent!

He jumps off the ladder and takes the Fragile Box, continuing to talk as he opens it with the help of his Swiss Army knife.

>   CHUCK (cont'd)
> Okay, people, now this package, I sent it before I left from
> Memphis. What's in here?

Out of the package Chuck pulls a TIMING CLOCK with a digital read-out.

>   CHUCK (cont'd)
> An egg timer.

He punches a button, stopping the clock.

>   CHUCK (cont'd)
> Eighty-seven hours! Eighty-seven hours to get from Memphis
> to Nicolai's house! That's an outrage!

Yuri is not nearly as embarrassed about this as perhaps he should be. Chuck displays the clock.

>   CHUCK (cont'd)
> What if it was your paycheck? Adoption papers? A kidney?
> Your new kidney. You want to be lying in a hospital, dying!
> Waiting for a transplant! You want to wait 87 hours for your
> kidney?!

Everyone shakes their heads. No, they don't.

>   CHUCK (cont'd)
> Eighty-seven hours is an eternity! We fight wars in 87 hours!

Whole nations have fallen in 87 hours!

Yuri mimics riding a bicycle, then says something in Russian which makes the assembled crowd stare at Chuck in a new way.

> CHUCK (cont'd)
> What? What?

> YURI
> I tell them, what do they expect? This man, when his truck broke down, he stole a boy's bicycle to do his delivery.

> CHUCK
> Borrowed, I borrowed it.
(then)
>> But you know what? I got those packages delivered! I did what it takes. And that's what we're going to do!

He points up at the clock.

> CHUCK (cont'd)
> And in three hours and four minutes, we're going to have every package on the Big Truck headed for the airport.

He points at a BIG TRUCK parked by the loading dock.

> YURI
> Impossible.

> CHUCK
> Impossible?

> YURI
> Trucks break down, traffic gets stuck in snow, drivers get lost.

Suddenly a DRIVER pulls in with a clean truck, all the letters properly painted. He jumps out and opens the rear doors, revealing that all his packages are neatly stacked.

CHUCK

Who is that?

Chuck strides toward the truck. Yuri scrambles to keep up.

YURI

Lev? A driver only.

CHUCK

Ask him how come he's back and the other drivers aren't.

Yuri and LEV BOLKONSKY exchange a few harsh words in Russian as Lev helps the Loaders unload his truck.

YURI

He says he sorts packages before he leaves office. Saves him half-hour, maybe more.

Chuck can't believe this.

CHUCK

What? You mean the other drivers DON'T sort their packages before they go? They don't plan their route? What is this? Why don't they?

Lev snorts something in Russian.

CHUCK (cont'd)

What did he say?

YURI

He is very rude, this fellow –

CHUCK

Tell me exactly what he said.

Lev looks directly at Chuck and speaks for himself.

> LEV

I say, why don't my farts smell sweet?

Chuck grins. Lev grins back.

> CHUCK

Well, Lev, that's a very good analogy.

Chuck turns to the rest of the office.

> CHUCK (cont'd)

And I tell you what, people, we're going to make this office smell like roses. And we're going to start by getting every package, from every truck, on the Big Truck before that clock hits all zeroes. Yes? Right?

He points to the clock, which switches from 03:00:00 to 02:59:59. He looks back at Lev and Yuri. Lev and Yuri speak at once.

> LEV

No problem.

> YURI

Impossible.

Chuck stares at Yuri, glances back at Lev. Chuck takes the clipboard from an astonished Yuri and hands it to Lev.

> CHUCK (cont'd)

Lev, you're in charge.

INT. FEDEX OFFICE MOSCOW LATER THAT DAY
The clock says 00:17:59.
The office is filled with trucks and activity. Packages are being sorted into sorting bags, which are loaded onto the Big Truck. Lev is talking on a cell phone.

CHUCK

Looking good, people, looking good! What we're doing here is
the future! This is running in front of the locomotive! Betting
the farm! Flying without a net! You snooze, you lose!

LEV

We have problem.

CHUCK

What? What is it?

LEV

Driver, he goes into department store in Red Square. He comes
out, no wheels.

CHUCK

What, are they flat?

LEV

No, not flat. Gone. Dasvidanya. It's Kremlin truck. Most
important one.

CHUCK

How far to Red Square?

LEV

Three kilometers.

CHUCK

No, no, no. In time.

LEV

Six, seven minutes.

CHUCK

Is that on the way to the airport?

                              LEV

    Yeah, sure. But we have one more truck still not in. A small
    truck, but still has packages.

Chuck thinks for a minute, then makes a decision.

                             CHUCK

    Okay, we'll do the sort in Red Square. Comrades! Get your
    boots and your babushkas! Follow me!

He leads them out of the office.

EXT. RED SQUARE MOMENTS LATER
Fyodor the driver and a Russian COP stand next to the FedEx truck,
its rims resting on the snow. Fyodor is drinking his vodka. Coming
towards us is the Big Truck, followed by another FedEx truck.
The two trucks roar up in the snow. Chuck and Lev jump out, followed by other workers and by the boy Nicolai carrying the TIMER
CLOCK that was in the Fragile Box. It says 00:09:15.
Chuck starts organizing the workers as they back up the trucks and
unload a folding table. Lev talks in Russian to the cop.

                             CHUCK

    Back that truck right up here!

Lev turns from the cop and speaks to Chuck.

                              LEV

    He says he can find the wheels for a thousand dollars U.S.

                             CHUCK

    Are you kidding me? How much for new wheels?

                              LEV

    Black market, one fifty U.S.

CHUCK

Tell him we'll give him a hundred-twenty-five for doing his
duty and apprehending our stolen property.

Lev grins and says something to the Cop in Russian.

CHUCK (cont'd)

Nicolai! Time!

NICOLAI

(in Russian)
Six minutes forty-five seconds!

CHUCK

Let's get cracking!

Chuck helps the loaders sort the packages while Lev calls the office
on the bulky cell phone he has slung over his shoulder. The workers
load the packages onto the two waiting trucks.

CHUCK (cont'd)

IP, IP, that's a P2, see by the code there?! Don't get snow on it
if you can help it! Looking good, people.
(to Lev)
Any word on the last truck?

LEV

Not yet.

At that moment the ALARM on Chuck's watch goes off. He checks the
time.

CHUCK

Have them patch me through to Memphis. 901-371-1354.

Lev speaks into his cell phone as Chuck keeps rallying the troops.

CHUCK (cont'd)
Keep going, comrades! The clock is running out! It's overtime, the game's on the line.

The Russians have no idea what Chuck is talking about. Lev hands Chuck the phone. We hear the voice of KELLY on an answering machine.

KELLY (V.O.)
This is Kelly. If you're calling for Chuck, please press 1. Otherwise, leave a message after the tone. Thanks.

CHUCK
Kelly, it's me. Pick up. Kelly. Pick up. Damn. Okay, look, you're not gonna believe this. I'm in the middle of Red Square – I'll try again when I get to Paris. Oh, can you get me a dental appointment? My tooth's killing me again.

As he talks Chuck takes in the scene: the FedEx trucks, the folding table in the snow, the – uh, oh – package going in the wrong truck.

CHUCK (cont'd)
Look, gotta go! But I'm coming home, I'm coming home.

As he hangs up, Lev comes up with some news.

LEV
Truck is in! I told them come to Red Square. We sort here, we make plane with all packages.

There's one thing Chuck has to know first.

CHUCK
Nicolai! Time!

Nicolai runs up with the clock. 00:00:58.

CHUCK (cont'd)

When that clock says zero, you go. I don't care if Lenin comes out of his tomb with a priority package!

LEV

What happen to flying without net?

In the background Nicolai is counting down the last seconds in Russian.

CHUCK

(as he gets into the Big Truck)

If we miss that plane, we could screw up the Memphis sort. And if we screw up the Memphis sort, well, that's the end of life as we know it.

Nicolai gets to zero.

NICOLAI

Blast off!

The workers SLAM the cargo doors on the Big Truck.

CHUCK

(to everyone)

Comrades! You did great!

(to Lev)

Listen, you're gonna be fine. Get 'em all on the truck tomorrow. Page me, let me know how the sort goes. Merry Christmas. Dasvidanya!

Chuck waves good-bye. Lev waves back as the Big Truck grinds into gear.

INT. BIG TRUCK MOSCOW MOMENTS LATER

The Big Truck pulls away from Red Square. We're on Chuck's face: the act is over. Chuck wipes his hand across his brow. He's done in.

Just then the last FedEx truck races by, headed into Red Square. Chuck watches it pass, knowing Lev was right: they could have made it.

INT. FEDEX MD-11 PARIS NIGHT LATER
Clear Plexiglas CONTAINERS are being loaded into the cargo hold of the plane. Through the Plexiglas we see cases of Mouton Cadet, big wheels of cheese, trays of Belon oysters. As the containers are wheeled on we hear the loaders speaking French. In the cockpit the pilots JACK and GWEN – are going down their checklists. Through the door comes Chuck.

> CHUCK
> I absolutely, positively, have to get to Memphis overnight.

> JACK
> Can't help you. Try UPS.

> CHUCK
> Jack – gotta be something wrong with our doctors, you keep getting certified to fly. Gwen, aren't you worried?

> GWEN
> Terrified.

> CHUCK
> We've got a 15-knot headwind, right? But we'll still make it, we're slotted for the sort?

> JACK
> We'll do our best.

> CHUCK
> Your 'best'? Hey, relentless is our goal. Never let up, right, Gwen?

Chuck may be kidding – a little. Jack and Gwen share a look as another FedEx Road Warrior named STAN BENSON gets on.

> STAN
>
> What do you expect, from the guy who stole a crippled kid's bicycle when his truck broke down?

> CHUCK
>
> Borrowed. I borrowed it. And he wasn't crippled.

Stan's got a bag full of baguettes and food and another bag full of gifts. He hands Gwen a small carved wooden effigy.

> STAN
>
> Straight from New Guinea. Keeps crocodiles away.

> GWEN
>
> Thanks. I've been needing this.

Stan hands Jack a long curved wooden stick.

> STAN
>
> Let me be the first to give you your penis gourd. Everybody's gonna be wearing them.

Stan turns to Chuck as Jack examines his penis gourd.

> STAN (cont'd)
>
> Sorry, Chuck, don't have one for you.

> CHUCK
>
> Course not. They don't make them in extra extra large.

The Loader slams the cargo door shut.

INT. FEDEX MD-11 NIGHT LATER

Stan breaks off a piece of baguette. Chuck's portable PC displays his Moscow report. We see a few doodles on the papers spread out from the FedEx pouch left on his seat. Stan fills a paper cup from a bottle wrapped in a sack. Chuck spreads cheese with his Swiss Army knife.

> STAN
>
> You missed the last truck by two minutes?

He hands Chuck a cup.

> CHUCK
>
> Seemed like less.

> STAN
>
> The plane wasn't that heavy. You could have dumped fuel, made up the time.

> CHUCK
>
> And then the next day, the last truck's four minutes late. Then six. Then ten. Then we're the U.S. Mail.

> STAN
>
> All I'm saying is, if you'd got all the trucks on the plane, those Russkies would be walking on water.

The restroom door opens and Gwen the pilot comes out. She gives the paper cups full of "grape juice" the gimlet eye.

> STAN (cont'd)
>
> Hey, don't give me that look. It's grape juice, right, Chuck?

> CHUCK
>
> I'd say a 1992, full-bodied grape juice.

> STAN
>
> (to Gwen)
>
> I'd offer you some but someone's got to drive the plane.

> GWEN
>
> I'll just say no, right?

Gwen is playing along, but there's something else on her mind. She switches gears, looking at Stan with sympathy.

> GWEN (cont'd)
> Listen, I've been meaning to ask, how's Mary?

Stan is suddenly dead serious.

> STAN
> Well, we still don't know. She went to the doctor yesterday. It hasn't metastasized, far as they can tell. So it's kind of just wait and see.

Gwen speaks simply and from the heart.

> GWEN
> I'm so sorry. Tell her I'll stop by to see her on my next layover. And you know, Stan, we're all thinking of her. And you.

> STAN
> Thanks.

Gwen lays her hand reassuringly on Stan's shoulder and walks back into the cockpit. Stan turns to Chuck. Chuck doesn't know what to say. Stan closes his PC.

> STAN (cont'd)
> Screw it...

Stan takes two pills – we don't know what they are, could be aspirin, could be whatever – then hands the bottle to Chuck, who takes two himself.

> STAN (cont'd)
> Let's go offline.

Chuck watches Stan put a mask over his eyes and lean back, trying to settle himself.

EXT. TARMAC FEDEX SUPERHUB MEMPHIS NIGHT
Chuck is on his cell phone.

> KELLY (V.O.)
> This is Kelly. If you're looking for Chuck...

Chuck clicks off. He's standing beside the MD-11 as LOADERS roll out the containers from the cargo hold. Stan comes up with his gear.

> CHUCK
> Look, I was thinking, there's a great doctor, down at Emory, in Atlanta. Took care of Frank Toretta's wife, you know Frank, from systems analysis? Played center field for us Labor Day?

Stan doesn't have a clue.

> CHUCK (cont'd)
> You know him. Look, it doesn't matter. His doctor's great. The best. I'll get you the number.

> STAN
> Thanks.

Stan's ebullience is gone. He looks groggy and depressed. They climb onto a cargo puller.

> CHUCK
> We'll beat this thing.

And the cargo puller whisks them away, toward the terminal.

INT. MEMPHIS STATE BIOLOGY BUILDING LATER THAT NIGHT
The clock in the hallway says 1:25. Chuck enter's Kelly's office: a small cubicle full of books, papers, and some specimen jars. There's a light on over the desk. A purse on the chair. A coffee cup still steaming. She's just been here.

INT. MEMPHIS STATE BIOLOGY BLDG NIGHT MOMENTS LATER
Chuck enters a LAB ROOM where a couple of GRAD STUDENTS work on
a project and another plays a video game on a computer.

                    CHUCK
    Anybody seen Kelly Frears?

                    STUDENT
    Xerox room. Copying her dissertation.

He gestures down the hall.

INT. MEMPHIS STATE BIOLOGY BLDG NIGHT MOMENTS LATER
Chuck walks down the hall toward where a WOMAN stands, her back
to us, using the XEROX MACHINE. The clock above her says 1:35. A
case of specimen jars is along the wall.
The woman is KELLY, hair up, glasses on, dressed in no-nonsense jeans.
We see her face in the green intermittent light. She examines each page
as it comes out, scanning the writing, making a quick note on one of
the charts. We hear the Ka-Chunk, Ka-Chunk of the machine.
For a long moment we are on Chuck's face as he stares at her. He's
just come from talking to Stan about Mary and, by implication, the
fragility of life. He's home from Russia. This is the woman he loves.
Kelly senses his presence and turns to face him. A smile lights her face.

                    KELLY
    It's you...

She comes into his arms. As they hug, in the b.g. we hear the Ka-
Chunk, Ka-Chunk of the copier. Chuck begins to move to it, a slow,
romantic dance to the beat of the Xerox. The machine stops. Kelly
pushes a button. It starts up again, and so does their dance.

INT. CHUCK/KELLY CONDO MEMPHIS NIGHT LATER
Half-dressed, Chuck lies asleep on the couch. The clock on the table
next to him reads 2:30. On TV we see late-night programming.
Kelly enters, eating from a plate of scrambled eggs. Now it's her turn

to stare at Chuck, at this driven man she's in love with. She reaches out to make him a little more comfortable. He stirs, then goes back to sleep.

INT. FEDEX SUPERHUB NEXT NIGHT
Eating pretzels out of a bag, Chuck heads up the stairs overlooking the Superhub. The wall clock says 21:58:30.
He walks through a COMMUNICATIONS ROOM.

> CHUCK
> Got the latest from Moscow?

The TECHNICIAN nods.

> TECHNICIAN
> Coming through now.

He nods into the conference room. Chuck pushes on into –

INT. FEDEX CONFERENCE ROOM SAME
A room dominated by a MAP OF THE WORLD. Through the windows we can see the vast machinery of the Memphis Hub and a row of air-planes. There's a large sign saying "Here Today, Gone Tomorrow" and two big digital clocks – one keeping time, the other counting down for that day's sort. On both clocks is the date: DECEMBER 23. Around the table are small computer terminals.
Chuck sits down and pulls up Moscow on the computer. It's not great news.
The clock ticks over to 21:59:00. The doors open. BECCA TWIGG – the business-like senior vice president for operations – and several other EXECUTIVES, including MAYNARD GRAHAM – an MBA systems type – as well as Stan, enter, talking among themselves. All the talk is fast and crisp.

> BECCA
> They off-loaded two demi's into a J-can and then tried to jam the J-Can on a 727?

Stan sits down by Chuck, whispers to him.

> STAN
>
> Heads up, pal.

This doesn't make Chuck relaxed.

> MAYNARD
>
> We re-routed Anchorage, so the can won't be WDL.

> BECCA
>
> That's reactive. We have to be proactive.

It's 21:59:45. As the clock hits 22:00:00 Becca turns to the BIG TV SCREEN. Precisely at the moment she begins to talk, MICK HATHAWAY, the European operations manager, materializes on it. "London" is superimposed on the screen.

> BECCA (cont'd)
>
> So why was Milan late, Mick?

> MICK
>
> One of the race horses coming from Ireland got colic and had to be off-loaded in Brussels. That put us six hours late into Charles DeGaulle. Customs had difficulty locating the dutiable items –

> BECCA
>
> Stan, can we get PPQ down to work with Milan customs?

> STAN
>
> We're already on it.

> BECCA
>
> Good, that's reactive. But let's look at our live animal policy. Maybe have a vet certify all our animals before they fly. That's proactive.

Becca hits a button. Mick disappears.

> BECCA (cont'd)

Chuck, Moscow?

> CHUCK

Moscow was averaging more than 36 hours between SIP and SOP. Load rates were under ten. Half the computers weren't on line because they didn't have the right adapters.

Everyone shares a look. Adapters.. What next?

> CHUCK (cont'd)

The drivers didn't sort their packages until they were on their trucks. I replaced the manager –

> MAYNARD

Says here he missed a truck the first day...
(checks the grid on his computer)
... two the second, one again today...

> CHUCK

They'd never missed less than six before.

> MAYNARD

You could have brought in someone from Memphis. Russia is priority one.

> CHUCK

Which is why we have to develop local staff. I figure that's being... proactive.

Chuck spins "proactive" lightly enough to take the brown-nosing off it. Becca's not that impressed.

> BECCA

People, getting from disastrous to pretty good is not what

49

we're about. We don't want a five percent failure rate. We want it zero.

Becca stares around the room.

> BECCA (cont'd)
> Anything else?

> STAN
> Malaysia's tanking. We've got systems problems, we've got malfunctions, we've got bad weather in the Pacific. We'll have a better picture over the next 36 hours.

> BECCA
> You better be ready to parachute someone in there.

She glares at Chuck, who smiles with as much enthusiasm as he can muster. Becca stands up. The formal part of the meeting is over.

> BECCA (cont'd)
> Okay, all you Santa's little helpers...

Her AIDE hands her a box. Becca walks around the table, passing out YELLOW GLOVES with red Christmas bows on them.

> BECCA (cont'd)
> This is the night we fancy executives remind ourselves what this company's all about. We're projecting two point eight million tonight. Let's go sort 'em.

INT. MEMPHIS SUPERHUB NIGHT LATER

Our executives work amid the army of EMPLOYEES sorting the rivers of Christmas packages that flow relentlessly into the Hub. Some still have ties on, others have on Christmas hats. It's incredibly complex; the work is demanding, intense. Like "Modern Times" on overdrive. Above them is a COUNTDOWN clock approaching 00:15:00.

We find Chuck as he flips packages over to be scanned. His back half to the chute, Chuck concentrates on the packages. Flips one, flips another, flips another... suddenly the next one is a TRAY OF KRISPY KREME DONUTS with Christmas sprinkles.

Then next to him is Kelly, wearing a temporary worker's badge and holding a sprig of mistletoe.

                              KELLY
        Merry Christmas.

She kisses him, then points to a package speeding by.

                         KELLY (cont'd)
        Missed one.

She flips the package. Then she grabs the tray and starts passing out the donuts. Chuck flips packages and watches her go down the line, exchanging greetings with Rasheed and others. Then she stops to comfort Stan in a simple genuine way.

The clock begins to flash: CRUNCH! CRUNCH!

                              BECCA
        Crunch time, people!

Chuck turns to the packages as the energy level ratchets up ever higher.

INT. KELLY'S MOM'S HOUSE NIGHT CHRISTMAS EVE
A carved turkey spilling off the platter is being passed around a dining room table. We hear the fading sounds of the Hub, then the hubbub of Christmas Eve dinner. By the table we see a GRANDFATHER CLOCK that says 7:30.

Chuck and Kelly are at the table with Kelly's EXTENDED FAMILY.

                           ANNE LARSON
        The turkey's a little dry, don't you think?

ANNE made the turkey. She doesn't think it's dry and no one in his

51

right mind would agree with her.

> CHUCK
>
> It's great.

Through the dining room door we can see a Christmas tree and another table set up for the KIDS. Everyone is in the midst of filling their plates and taking their first bites. The conversation is quick and over-lapping, bits and snatches of dialogue.
Chuck's plate is full and getting fuller. VIRGINIA LARSON passes Chuck a bowl of fruit salad drenched in white goo.

> MORGAN STOCKTON
>
> How many'd you do last night?

Morgan takes a sip from a can of Pabst Blue Ribbon.

> KELLY
>
> (re: the Waldorf salad)
> It's solid mayonnaise.

> CHUCK
>
> Two point nine.

Ignoring Kelly, Chuck takes a big spoonful of gooey salad onto his already full plate.

> MOM
>
> You've got to be in the market for some more candied yams.

She spoons some onto Chuck's plate. Kelly's eyebrow goes up, but there's no stopping Chuck.

> MORGAN STOCKTON
>
> Two point nine! Got to be the record.

> CHUCK
>
> Love those marshmallows.

KELLY

When I was there we broke two million and thought we'd hung
the moon.

MORGAN STOCKTON

What'd they do the first day?

DENNIS LARSON

Twelve –

JOE WALLY

Twelve thousand?

DENNIS LARSON

No, twelve.

CHUCK

Yeah, and they did the sort on a card table –

DENNIS LARSON

Fred Smith had that card table bronzed –

KELLY

Come on –
Dennis is not always to be believed.

DENNIS LARSON

Swear to God. It's in his office today.

Kelly looks at Chuck, who grins and shrugs: could be.

CHUCK

You oughta see that new Anchorage hub. The perfect marriage
of technology and systems management. Absolutely state-of-
the-art.

MORGAN STOCKTON

Speaking of marriage, Chuck, when are you going to make an

honest woman out of our Kelly here?

Chuck holds up his watch. He and Kelly have made a game out of the family's pressure to get married.

CHUCK
Fourteen minutes into dinner. A new record.

Kelly holds out her hand to Chuck.

KELLY
Five bucks. I told you it'd be Morgan.

MORGAN STOCKTON
Me? What did I do?

CHUCK
Don't worry, Morgan. It's just that she's still getting over her marriage to the parolee –

KELLY
He was a lawyer –

LISA MADDEN
Remember when he fell on the sidewalk at the wedding reception and broke his shoulder – ?

KELLY
Probably holding the door open for me.

RALPH WALLY
Aunt Kelly was married before – ?

MORGAN STOCKTON
How long was she married to that guy – ?

KELLY

He wasn't that bad –

CHUCK

So anyway, after the parolee –

KELLY

– lawyer –

CHUCK

– she's not sure she wants to marry a guy who wears a beeper to bed.

JOE WALLY

What do you attach it to, hoss?

Chuck helps himself to the dressing.

JOE WALLY (cont'd)

You wear it to bed, sure hope it's one of those vibrating kinds.

MOM

Your beeper vibrates?

Mom's not quite up to speed. Kelly tries to stave off further embarrassment.

KELLY

Come on, guys –

Chuck tries to chew instead of laugh, but when he takes a bite he winces. That damn tooth. Mom's suddenly very concerned.

ANNE LARSON

Did you hit an olive pit? I thought I took them all out.

                              CHUCK
        No, it's fine. Fine.

Chuck's BEEPER goes off. Do we laugh or what? Everyone looks to
Kelly for guidance, but she is absolutely deadpan, so everyone pretends to have something very important to do.

                          ANNE LARSON
        Karo syrup? You substituted karo syrup for the molasses in the
        pecan pie?

                         WENDY LARSON
        Dollars to donuts you can't tell the difference.

Chuck checks the number. Kelly catches his eye: oh no. But from
Chuck's look back we know: oh yes.

INT. BEDROOM MOMENTS LATER
Coats are scattered on two twin beds. Chuck and Kelly sit opposite
each other, with their Filofaxes. In the b.g. we see the kids opening
their Christmas presents.

                              KELLY
        Okay, I'll cancel Saturday –

                              CHUCK
        Don't. If I'm here, I'm here. If I'm not, I'm not.

                              KELLY
        Chuck. It's canceled. But you gotta be here for New Year's Eve.

                              CHUCK
        I'll be here. Malaysia shouldn't be that bad.

She stares at him.
                          CHUCK (cont'd)
        I promise. Now when do you defend your dissertation?

KELLY

January 12.

CHUCK

I'll move the South America thing. But that means I'll have to do it January 3rd or 4th. Then head out again on the 13th.

KELLY

Just so long as you're here New Year's Eve.

CHUCK

You got it.

They close up their Filofaxes.

KELLY

What about our Christmas? I've got a present for you.

CHUCK

We'll have to do it in the car.

EXT. FEDEX SUPERHUB LATER THAT NIGHT
At the main entrance cars and trucks come and go by an entry kiosk. In the b.g. we see planes. It's been raining. A black Jeep Cherokee pulls up, then veers off to the side. We hear Elvis singing Christmas carols from the car radio carrying us to:

INT. JEEP CHEROKEE SAME
Chuck sits in the passenger seat, trying to get a PACKAGE open, but the ribbon is too tight and he can't get it off. In the backseat we see some WRAPPING PAPER and other PRESENTS.

CHUCK

What is this ribbon – thousand-pound test? Hand me my keys. She hands him the car keys with the Swiss Army knife attached. Chuck pulls out the appropriate blade and cuts the ribbon. Out of the package he pulls a box. Chuck hesitates and glances at Kelly.

                            KELLY
    Go on.

Chuck opens it. Inside is an antique gold POCKET WATCH.

                            CHUCK
    It's terrific.

                            KELLY
    My grandfather used it on the Southern Pacific.

Chuck opens the watchcase. There's a tiny picture of Kelly mounted
in the case. What a great gift.

                            CHUCK
    I took this picture.

He starts to set the watch.

                        CHUCK (cont'd)
    I'll always keep this on Memphis time. Kelly time.

There's a tender moment between them, then he gets the slightest grin.

                        CHUCK (cont'd)
    You haven't said anything about your presents. Is there a
    problem?
    Well...

                            KELLY
    No... the journal is great.

She picks up a LEATHER DATEBOOK. There's also a BEEPER and some
semi-cheesy HAND TOWELS in a flat box.

                            CHUCK
    How about the beeper?

Kelly's going to let him off the hook. She keeps talking about the journal.

> KELLY
>
> Real leather. Look how it's organized.

> CHUCK
>
> So you didn't like the beeper?

> KELLY
>
> No, no. I love my beeper. It's not that loud, though, is it?

> CHUCK
>
> No way. You can program it. It vibrates, it lights up –

> KELLY
>
> It's one great beeper.

> CHUCK
>
> How about the hand towels?

> KELLY
>
> I love 'em. Whenever I wash my hands I'll think of you.

> CHUCK
>
> Great. Great. I'm glad you liked them. Well, gotta go.

He kisses her.

> CHUCK (cont'd)
>
> Merry Christmas.

He gets out of the car and starts to walk away.

> KELLY
>
> Chuck?

Chuck turns, he's got something up his sleeve.

KELLY (cont'd)

Keys.

Chuck pats his pocket. Right. Keys. He comes back to the car reaches into his pocket, and hands her the keys with the Swiss Army knife. As he does he pretends to find something else.

CHUCK

Oh, look, another present for you.

He takes it out of his pocket. It's a small package, a very small, beautifully wrapped package. A RING PACKAGE. The other gifts were just for fun, but this –
Kelly stares at it. She knows what it is but part of her doesn't want to know.

CHUCK (cont'd)

I almost forgot.

And of course he didn't.

CHUCK (cont'd)

There was one date we didn't set.

KELLY

Chuck –

Chuck's a little nervous about this anyway, but Kelly's confusion makes him back-pedal.

CHUCK

You know what? This isn't an open-in-the-car kind of present.

He starts to take it back, but that's not what she wants either.

CHUCK (cont'd)

Not like hand towels, which were a joke, by the way.

                          KELLY
    I just – I'm terrified –

She can't put her feelings into words. Maybe it has something to do
with living a life where you have Christmas in the car.

                          CHUCK
    Look, hold onto it, we'll open it New Year's Eve.

They kiss through the open window of the car.

                       CHUCK (cont'd)
    I'll be right back.

Kelly watches him walk away, toward the kiosk. Without turning
around Chuck waves to her.

INT. FEDEX MD-11 NIGHT HOURS LATER
The pocket watch Kelly gave Chuck is on the table next to his seat. It
vibrates. Vibrates again. Chuck is sleeping, a mask on his eyes, ear-
phones on. Suddenly the plane shakes violently! The CD player falls
off Chuck's lap. Chuck wakes up, startled and disoriented. Takes the
mask off his eyes.
Still groggy, Chuck stands up as AL, the replacement Captain, swings
down from the bunk opposite the bathroom and heads for the coffee
pot.

                          CHUCK
    Where are we?
                           AL
    Somewhere over the Pacific Ocean.

                          CHUCK
    You pilots. You're funny.

Chuck enters the cockpit, where KEVIN and BLAINE are at the controls. Lightning flashes, coming up from the clouds below. Kevin

takes note of the somewhat bleary-eyed Chuck. As he and Chuck talk we hear Blaine trying to raise Tahiti on the radio.

>   CHUCK (cont'd)
>   What was that? Little turbulence from Santa's sleigh and those
>   eight tiny reindeer?

Boom! We shake again.

>   KEVIN
> (deadpan)
>   What was what?

>   BLAINE
>   Tahiti Control, Tahiti Control, FedEx 88, FedEx 88, over...

But the answer is only static.

>   KEVIN
>   Give it another hour. We're still too far out.

Chuck glances at the radar screen, which is thick with clouds.

>   CHUCK
>   Look at all that.

>   KEVIN
>   Eight hundred miles of tropical depression.

>   BLAINE
>   We've been flying around it for an hour.

Al appears with some coffee for the crew.

>   AL
>   You'll need a fork for this coffee.

Boom! Coffee splatters. Chuck catches his balance.

> BLAINE
>
> I've never been out of Comm this long.

Blaine goes back on the radio, trying to raise Tahiti Control. Boom! The plane shakes again. Even harder this time. Al sits down in the jump seat.

> AL
>
> Have you tried the low altitude frequency?

Blaine switches the dial.

> BLAINE
>
> Tahiti Control, FedEx 88 –

Nothing but static.

> AL
>
> Better buckle up, Chuck. Could get really bumpy.

Chuck heads back out of the cockpit.

INT. FEDEX MD-11 LAVATORY MOMENTS LATER
Chuck lays his wristwatch on the sink. The bowl is full of water. Boom! Another bit of turbulence shivers the water. Chuck splashes some water on his face, then stares at his teeth for a moment. He reaches into his mouth, fingers a tooth, winces slightly. Then he pops a couple of pills.

BOOM!
AN EXPLOSION RIPS THROUGH THE PLANE! This isn't turbulence! The basin of water explodes out of the sink. Chuck is thrown out the door of the lavatory! The plane lurches violently!

The plane is in a steep dive! It shakes violently! There's major decompression! Gear flies everywhere! Smoke! Chaos! Al struggles to help Chuck with his oxygen mask.

All around him packages fly! Smoke blows from the cargo hold! In the cockpit we see all the emergency lights flashing.

                              AL
          Seat belt!

Chuck struggles into his seat and fastens his belt.

Lightning flashes outside the window! Al yanks at a compartment labeled LIFE RAFT.

Chuck glances in the cockpit. Red lights are flashing all over the control panels! The other three pilots have their smoke goggles and life jackets on. They're fighting the controls.

We hear snatches of the pilots going through emergency check lists. They still have no radio contact! The plane is in a steep dive!

Al jerks the life raft out of the compartment and jams it in Chuck's hands. He heads to the cockpit.

Chuck sits strapped in his seat, squeezing the life raft for dear life.

He looks down on the floor on the left side of the cabin.

His life vest.

Back to Chuck. What should he do?

He looks to the right side of the cabin.

Rattling around on the floor near the lavatory is the gold pocket watch.

Chuck looks to the raft. Looks to the watch.

Chuck slowly undoes his seat belt.

He moves toward the gold watch.

Whap!!

Violent turbulence throws Chuck to the floor.

Still holding tightly onto his life raft, he scrambles across the floor to the watch.

He grabs the watch quickly, shoves it into his pocket.

The plane is shaking and buffeting more violently now.

Chuck grabs onto the cargo net and slowly grapples his way across to get his life vest.

The plane is buffeted again.

The cargo container behind Chuck snaps loose and slams into the first cargo container! A portion of the cargo net breaks free, flinging Chuck halfway towards the cockpit door.

IN THE COCKPIT

Al turns around sees Chuck dangling helplessly from the cargo net. Undoing his seat belt, he takes a step towards Chuck.

                              AL
        Chuck! Life vest!

Thwapp!!! The plane drops 300 feet.

Both Chuck and Al are flung to the ceiling.

Al cracks his head on the overhead instrument panel. He crumples to the floor holding his head, bleeding profusely.

The plane banks violently to the right.

The cargo container behind Chuck's left shoulder rips open; packages tumble onto the floor.

Al lies across the floor by the lavatory, barely conscious. He holds his bleeding head.

Chuck looks at Al. Looks at the cockpit. What can he do? Through the window the ocean rushes up at us.

KABOOM! With a terrible impact, the plane hits the water!

The plane catapults!

The right engine grabs the ocean, flipping the fuselage around. The plane splits open! Waves blast through the cockpit!

Chuck is shot out into the water! The raft billows open in front of him! The huge wing with the engine attached tilts over, right at him, jet engine still blowing! It crashes into the water only a few feet away! Swells rise and fall. WHOOSH! The water catches on fire! Flames lick at Chuck!

Riding down a swell right next to him is... the raft. Chuck struggles toward it. The wing sinks beside him! The fire is only a few feet away! With all his strength Chuck slides into the raft as it rides the big waves. Wrapping his arm around the lashing inside, he holds himself inside the raft. Rain beats down. Lightning flashes. The sky is lit by the burning plane. Chuck yells at the top of his lungs.

CHUCK

AL?!

Maybe, just maybe, over the raging wind and the fire we hear a response. Chuck tries to paddle but the swells sweep him away.

EXT. OCEAN LATER THAT NIGHT
Lit occasionally by lightning flashes, Chuck struggles to hang on.

EXT. OCEAN STILL LATER THAT NIGHT
The rain falls steadily, the swells are even bigger. Chuck is exhausted, disoriented, cold; fear is on his face. Above him the dark sky crackles with lightning!

EXT. OCEAN LONG SHOT STILL LATER
Almost lost in the giant swells, a tiny bit of yellow – Chuck's raft – rides out the storm.
Suddenly, the raft scrapes on something solid.

EXT. ROCKY POINT NIGHT SAME
Half passed out, Chuck jolts awake. What the hell? The raft spins, caught on a coral reef. Rip! One of the floats is torn out! Lightning flashes again! Rising above the point like a broken obelisk is a steep rocky peak.
Dazed, confused, half in the raft, half on the rock, Chuck can't believe what he sees. Is it real? Is it a dream? He clings to the rocks and stares into the stormy darkness.
The lightning flashes again, bathing Chuck's face in light. Through the rain Chuck sees the distinctive peak, a white carpet of beach at its foot. It's shrouded in rain, but it's real.

EXT. PEAK DISSOLVE NIGHT/DAY
We stay on the peak through darkness into dawn as the rain dwindles to a drizzle. We TILT DOWN and see –

EXT. LAGOON DAWN WIDE
Chuck dragging the raft through the calm lagoon, toward the narrow spit of beach. In the foreground, waves crash and break on the rocks and the surrounding reef, which holds back the angry sea.

EXT. BEACH DAWN MOMENTS LATER
Bone-weary and disoriented, Chuck drags the remains of the raft up onto the beach and collapses into it.

EXT. BEACH DAY LATER
The sun shines bright and strong in the now clear blue sky.

EXT. BEACH DAY SAME
Sunlight hits Chuck's face and he comes groggily awake. Sitting up, he sees something down the SANDY POINT. Squinting, he looks again.

EXT. SANDY POINT DAY MOMENTS LATER
Still disoriented, Chuck staggers down the sandy spit. One of his socks is missing. A FEDEX BOX lies washed up on the beach. Mechanically, Chuck picks it up, brushes off the sand, not really conscious of what he's doing.
The package brings it all back: the last moments on the plane, the crash, the storm. Chuck looks around, and we look with him. Palm groves and rubber trees lead back into a JUNGLE climbing up a steep, rocky hillside. Jutting out into the shallows of the lagoon, is LIMPET POINT. Looking the other way, down the far side of Sandy Point, is another cliff, LANDING BEACH POINT. Chuck yells into the jungle.

                              CHUCK
        Hello? Hello?

The only answer is the rustling of the breeze in the palm trees, the lapping of the gentle waves on the sand and the crashing of the big breakers out on the reef.

                          CHUCK (cont'd)
        Anybody!?

Again, silence. Chuck looks out to sea, then up into the clearing sky.

EXT. BEACH DAY MOMENTS LATER

Chuck turns the raft over and props it up for some shade. Taking inventory, he checks his beeper. Water runs out of it. So important yesterday, so useless today. He sets it on the FedEx box.

He reaches into his pocket. The antique watch Kelly gave him is still there. He opens it up. The watch has stopped. Kelly time is no more. He stares at Kelly's picture. Yesterday the real Kelly had given it to him. The memory fills him with determination. Got to get out of here. Got to get home.

EXT. BEACH DAY MOMENTS LATER

Chuck finishes writing the last letter of H E L P in the sand with his foot. He kicks off his sandy sock, but the beach is hot on his feet. He stares up at the sky, the clear, blue, very empty sky. Rescuers should be coming for him. But where are they?

EXT. BEACH DAY LATER

Clothed only in his T-shirt, Chuck sits under his shelter. His other clothes hang drying from branches. He stares out to sea, then up into the sky. He takes the watch and stares at Kelly's picture for a long time. The reality of what's happened is still sinking in. Finally he sets Kelly's picture back down on the box in the sunlight beside him and turns his gaze back out to sea.

EXT. BEACH LATER THAT DAY

Kelly's picture is now in shadow. We pan up from it to Chuck, who hasn't moved. He licks his lips. He's thirsty, but he's afraid to leave the beach. What if someone comes while he's gone?

EXT. BEACH NIGHT LATER

Chuck lies in the raft in the moonlight, brushed by moonshadows of swaying palms. His sweater is his pillow. His eyes are wide open. He can't sleep. Suddenly: THUD! There's a sound in the jungle. Chuck jumps, terrified. What the hell was that? Chuck stares into the jungle, but all he sees are moonshadows.

He puts his head back down. He's thirsty and scared. THUD! There it
is again. Dammit!
He stares out at –

EXT. OCEAN NIGHT SAME
All he can see is the moonlight on the water, the stars, and the line of
white breakers crashing on the reef. Dammit! Where the hell is every-
body?

EXT. BEACH EARLY THE NEXT MORNING
Wearing only his T-shirt, Chuck stands over the remains of the
H E L P. All but the tops of the letters have been washed away by the
tide.

EXT. BEACH DAY HALF HOUR LATER
Chuck finishes writing H E L P again, this time more permanently –
with driftwood and rocks on the lip of the beach, above the high tide
line.

EXT. LAGOON DAY MOMENTS LATER
A FedEx box floats in the lagoon. Chuck comes toward us, his pants
rolled up, carrying two FedEx boxes under his arm.
As Chuck picks up the new box, THUD! Another of those sounds that
disturbed him last night. Chuck stares up at the jungle and sees a BIG
ROCK standing on end at the edge of the jungle, amidst a pile of other
rocks.

EXT. BEACH DAY MOMENTS LATER
Chuck dumps the FedEx boxes down on the sand and carefully sorts
them by priority into two stacks. THUD! There's that sound again. But
this time as Chuck looks up he sees a COCONUT rolling down toward
the beach. A coconut. Hmmm.

EXT. BIG ROCK MOMENTS LATER
Chuck dumps an armful of green coconuts down in the loose rocks by
Big Rock. He picks one up, shakes it. Milk sloshes inside. He's so
thirsty. But how to open it?

He throws the coconut down on the rocks, hard. But the coconut just bounces away.

EXT. BIG ROCK MOMENTS LATER
A coconut is wedged between two rocks. Taking another rock in his hand, Chuck slams the rock down on the coconut, but nothing happens. He SLAMS it down again, but the rock glances off the coconut and SMASHES into another rock. The rock in his hand SPLINTERS, cutting Chuck's hand. OWWW! He sucks the blood away.
Then he thinks for a minute. The shard of rock in his hand is sharp. He tests it against his finger. He gets an idea, the same idea that came to primitive man when he discovered stone tools.

EXT. BIG ROCK MOMENTS LATER
Chuck saws at the green husk with the rough sharp edge of his stone knife. Then he wedges the rock into the green husk and hacks and pulls the husk off, revealing the brown nut inside.
Holding the nut against a rock, he tries to break it open by striking it with another rock, but DAMN! The nut breaks to smithereens!
Coconut milk splatters everywhere! Chuck tries to scoop some of the milk up, but it soaks away into the sand. No!

EXT. BIG ROCK MOMENTS LATER
Using a round rock as a hammer, Chuck gently taps a thin shard of rock into the eye of a coconut. Once the makeshift drill is in, he twists it gently, then, ah ha! The nut is open!
He pulls out the drill, then gulps at the milk of the coconut. The milk runs down his lips.

EXT. BIG ROCK MOMENTS LATER
A broken coconut shell is tossed onto a pile of other broken shells. We move up to find Chuck rubbing the milk off his lips. His thirst is quenched. He stares down the beach.

HIS VIEW LIMPET POINT SAME
The lagoon laps at the rocks. What's beyond it?

EXT. BIG ROCK DAY SAME
Chuck turns and looks down the beach the other way.

HIS VIEW LANDING BEACH POINT SAME
The waves wash up on the rocks behind Sandy Point. No telling what's past there either.

EXT. BIG ROCK DAY SAME
Chuck thinks for a moment. Time to go exploring.

EXT. LAGOON DAY MOMENTS LATER
His shirt draped over his head for shade, his pants rolled up, coconuts stuffed into his sweater, Chuck wades in the shallows toward Limpet Point. In the water we see crabs and fish. On a rock we see mollusks.
He's chewing on a coconut, but his tooth hurts. He tosses the piece of coconut away. Behind him we see the beach and the palm grove. He rounds Limpet Point.

EXT. CAVE ENTRANCE DAY LATER
The shadows lengthen. He passes a CAVE ENTRANCE, a narrow slit tucked up in the rocks at the high tide line. Up above the cave entrance, high on the cliff, is another cave mouth with a palm tree growing out of it.
Chuck wades around the cave entrance and confronts a sheer rock wall where the waves beat. No exit here. Damn!

EXT. LANDING BEACH POINT DAY LATER
It's late in the day now. Chuck wades out around Sandy Point, stepping gingerly on the rock and coral. He comes face to face with another rock wall, extending out into deep blue water. No way out that way either. But there is something else, another FedEx box, wedged in the rocks. Chuck picks it up and turns it over. Painted on it are – WINGS!
Wings almost exactly like the ones we saw in Russia, only these are gold and have a holiday feeling. Intrigued, Chuck stares at them.

EXT. CAMPSITE DAY MOMENTS LATER
Chuck hobbles up to camp on his sore feet, sets the Angel Wing Box
down on top of the other boxes, then sits down and examines his feet,
which are scraped and sore from walking on the coral.

EXT. BEACH DUSK LATER CLOSE-UP
Chuck's stone knife saws away on his pants in the moonlight, cutting
them off at the knee.

EXT. BEACH WIDE DAY SAME
Chuck saws with great determination.

EXT. BEACH EARLY THE NEXT MORNING
Chuck tears at the elastic in the legs of his underwear, then wraps the
elastic around the cut-off bottom of his pants, securing it to his foot.
He stuffs some palm leaves inside, then does the same inside the sock
that covers his other foot.

EXT. BIG ROCK MOMENTS LATER
We see Chuck's newly covered feet pass Big Rock and we WIDEN as he
heads into the jungle.

EXT. JUNGLE DAY MOMENTS LATER
Coconuts again slung in his sweater, Chuck makes his way through
the jungle, pushing aside undergrowth and rubber tree leaves.

EXT. MOUNTAIN LATER
Chuck struggles up a steep embankment of loose rock.

EXT. STONY SADDLE DAY LATER
Chuck pulls himself up. Below him he can see the beach where he
wrote H E L P and then, as we PAN UP, he can see the summit where
he has to go.
Chuck pulls out a coconut, unplugs a twig from the hole, takes a
drink, then heads up the rocky slope leading up toward the peak. It's
tough going. He slips and slides, muttering to himself.

EXT. ISLAND WIDE

The small figure of Chuck limps and stumbles, almost to the top of the summit.

EXT. SUMMIT DAY LATER

Breathing hard, Chuck pulls himself up to the summit. The sun is low in the sky. He looks to each point on the compass. On three sides the waves break against steep, hostile cliffs. On the fourth, a reef encloses the cove where he came from. No way on. No way off. He's on an island, without sign of habitation or anything human.

                              CHUCK

    Jesus.

It's the shock of recognition. A plea for help. A soft cry of despair. Chuck stares out to sea, into the lonely nothingness of sky and ocean. He looks down at the waves crashing on the rocky point where he came ashore. Suddenly he sees a glint. Something yellowish. What the – ?

EXT. STONY SADDLE DAY MOMENTS LATER

The light is fading. Chuck scrambles down the rocks, slipping and sliding, barely keeping his balance.

EXT. JUNGLE DUSK MOMENTS LATER

Chuck runs through the darkening jungle, leaves and branches whipping at his face.

EXT. LAGOON DUSK MOMENTS LATER

In the dark light of sunset Chuck splashes into the lagoon.
He wades out to the Rocky Point. A LIFEJACKET is stuck on the inside of the reef, just beyond where the waves crash with rhythmic, daunting booms.
There's a body in the lifejacket. A body in a pilot's uniform. Covered with crabs. Chuck stares at it for a moment, not sure what to do. He doesn't want to touch the body. He looks around for someone to help. But there's no one there. Whatever has to be done, Chuck will have to do it himself.

Chuck gingerly tugs at the body, trying to free it from the rocks. The crabs scurry away.

EXT. ROCKY POINT DUSK UNDERWATER SAME
We see Al, face down, hair floating, very gray and very dead.

EXT. LAGOON MAGIC HOUR WIDE
It's almost night. Chuck drags Al by the lifejacket across the lagoon.

EXT. BIG ROCK NEXT MORNING
A big mound of sand has been piled up next to Big Rock. Sweating, Chuck finishes digging Al's grave with the liferaft paddle.
A few feet away Al's body lies covered with palm fronds. Chuck goes over to it. Crabs have gathered again. He shoos them.

CHUCK
Get the hell away!

Awkwardly – this is hard – Chuck reaches under the palm fronds and feels around, then removes Al's beeper. It's as waterlogged as Chuck's was. Then he disengages a pilot's MINI MAG FLASHLIGHT from its belt holster, sets it aside. Then, feeling under Al, he takes out his WALLET. Inside the wallet are some Australian and American money, credit cards, Al's driver's and pilot's licenses, a photograph of him with two sons.
Chuck stares at the photograph for a long moment. He checks the license.

CHUCK (cont'd)
Albert... Miller. Albert Miller.

EXT. BEACH DAY MOMENTS LATER
Al's shoes drag in the sand as Chuck pulls the body to the grave. He lays it down in the grave, pulls the head toward one end. But the feet still stick out a little. Damn.
Chuck gently crosses Al's arms over his chest, then brushes some sand off Al's forehead. He tries to close the eyes, but they won't stay shut, so he lays some palm fronds over Al's face.

He goes down to the other end of the grave and starts to take off Al's shoes.

> CHUCK
>
> Sorry, Al, I need your shoes.

He has to wrestle with the legs to make them fit into the grave. It's maddeningly hard to do. Breathing hard, Chuck struggles, then finally wedges the feet into the grave.

EXT. BEACH DAY WIDE
Chuck shovels sand into the grave with the paddle.

EXT. BIG ROCK MOMENTS LATER ECU
Using a sharpened stone, Chuck carves the last of the inscription on the Big Rock, which serves as a headstone. A MILLER 6 14 50 – 12 25 95.

EXT. BIG ROCK DAY SAME
Chuck steps back and regards the headstone and the newly dug grave. He speaks haltingly, searching back into the rag and bone shop of his memory, trying to do justice to the man under the sand.

> CHUCK
>
> Ashes to ashes, dust to dust. We bring nothing into the world,
> we can't take anything out of it.
>
> (beat)
>
> I don't know what to say, Al.
>
> (beat)
>
> I guess that's it.

EXT. CAMPSITE DAY LATER
Chuck tries on Al's shoes. They're too tight.

EXT. CAMPSITE DAY MOMENTS LATER
Chuck saws at the toes with his stone knife, peeling off the leather. Then he slips his feet inside. The toes stick out the front a little, but he has shoes now.

EXT. BEACH LATER

Using his foot shod in his new shoes, Chuck puts an exclamation point on H E L P. Things are serious now. Death is in the air. He looks up into the sky. It's empty. Damn it! Why haven't they come?

EXT. BEACH NIGHT

Clouds cross the moon. The night is black. Click. A light comes on. Chuck is sitting in the raft. He turns the light off. Black again. Click. The light comes on again. He shines the light on Kelly's picture. He stares at it for a long time, then turns the light off. Click. It comes on again. He stares again at Kelly's photograph.
Click. The light goes off. Into the blackest black we've ever seen.

EXT. JUNGLE NEXT MORNING

Chuck squats over a hastily dug cat hole behind a bush, straining from the dueling effects of the coconut: laxative from the milk, constipation from the meat. The paddle stands by a tree. Ooooh, Gilligan never told us this!

EXT. JUNGLE A FLAT ROCK LATER THAT DAY

A puddle of dirty water is trapped in a tiny hollow. Chuck flops down next to it. He tries to scoop up some water in his hands, but he just splashes it around. He licks his fingers. Mainly what's there is mud, but it's wet. Chuck hesitates for a moment. If he's going to survive, he has to drink it, so he gets down on his stomach and laps at the mud with his tongue. Like an animal.

EXT. JUNGLE DAY MOMENTS LATER

Water shimmers in a delicate leaf as Chuck very carefully starts to drain it off into a coconut shell. With total concentration he pours the water into the shell. Then he gently holds the shell up to another leaf. This is how he will get water: painstakingly, drop by drop.

EXT. BIG ROCK DAY

Chuck breaks a stick over his knee, then tests the point on the broken end. Hmmmm. Sharp enough.

EXT. LAGOON DAY

Holding the sharpened stick, Chuck wades at low tide, looking for
fish. Suddenly a shadow flashes by, glinting in the sunlight. Chuck
clumsily hurls the spear! But it ricochets off the water and floats away.
Chuck plunges after the fish with his bare hands. The fish reverses
direction. Chuck falls to his hands and knees in the shallows and
comes up sputtering.

Suddenly a school of fish swims by him, moving in unison, like one
creature, splitting around Chuck like mercury. He grabs at them desperately. Nothing.

EXT. BEACH SUNSET

Chuck sits on the beach, chewing mechanically on a handful of seaweed. It looks awful. He looks awful. It's really sinking in: no one is
coming. There will be no rescue. He's stuck here, alone.

EXT. ISLAND NIGHT

Stars burn furiously. The sky is clear now, and we look up into an
infinity of space. We TILT DOWN and find our tiny island in the midst
of the vast ocean, and on the beach in the moonlight we see Chuck,
staring at the stars.

He gets up, walks down to the beach, and stands in the shallows. We
are behind him, over his shoulder. And as he stares out at the stars we
hear the sound of Chuck pissing into the ocean.

Suddenly he stares out past the reef. There, on the horizon, is a LIGHT,
winking at him. What the hell is that? A star?

He stares at it really hard. It's not a star. Too low for a plane. It's a
ship!

He runs back up the beach, stumbling in the sand. He grabs the mag
light and runs back down to the beach, waving it and yelling at the
top of his lungs.

                              CHUCK

Hey! Hey!

Then he squints. Where did that light go? There it is! But it flickers,
then... blackness.

82

He flicks off the penlight, stares into the darkness. Nothing. Wait! Someone is out there! He'll save himself!! Now!!

He runs back to his life raft, kicks out the stick propping it up and turns it over.

EXT. BEACH EARLY NEXT MORNING

Chuck wades into the water, pulling the raft, which is loaded with coconuts for water and food. Holding the raft steady, he climbs in.

EXT. LAGOON LATER THAT MORNING

Chuck puts on his life jacket. Steadying the raft, he begins to paddle toward the reef.

HIS VIEW THE REEF

The waves pound on the reef ahead of him. This is going to be tough.

EXT. RAFT MOMENTS LATER

Chuck approaches the reef break. He glances back at the island behind him.

EXT. REEF MOMENTS LATER

Boom. Swoosh. The waves break with incredible power. The waves are BIG, much bigger than they seemed from the beach.

EXT. RAFT MOMENTS LATER

Chuck pauses, stunned by their size, their power. But he's got no choice, he's got to do it.

Chuck positions the raft, trying to time the action of the waves. It's going to take an act of total commitment.

Suddenly, he paddles furiously, but it's too late. Desperate, he back-paddles to escape the crashing wave. This is impossible.

                                CHUCK
        Damn you! Do it!

He waits, waits, waits, then paddles in with all his strength! The raft cuts into an enormous wave. Chuck paddles up the rising side of the

wave, poises on the crest, then paddles down the backside.
He's made it! Then he looks up and –

HIS VIEW HUGE WAVE
A HUGE WAVE looms right before him, so much bigger than the one he just did. This is the real thing.

EXT. RAFT SAME
Chuck paddles feverishly, trying to beat the wave coming at him!
BOOM! The wave CRASHES into the raft! It's ripped to shreds!

EXT. OCEAN UNDERWATER SAME
Chuck goes under! The wave tumbles him violently! The waves pound and crash, sweep him against the sharp coral. He's cut! Blood clouds in the water from his leg. The waves crash again!

EXT. OCEAN DAY MOMENTS LATER
Chuck breaks the surface, gasping for breath. Another wave is poised above him! BOOM! It crashes down again!

EXT. ISLAND DAY WIDE MOMENTS LATER
We see Chuck limping toward us, stumbling, dragging the remains of the raft. It's all he can do to take a single step. He stumbles up the beach and as he passes, hyperventilating, we can see the wound in his thigh, a deep, nasty coral cut.

EXT. BEACH DAY MOMENTS LATER
Chuck limps up on the beach, trying to hold the wound together with his hand. He rips the seam of his pants to expose the wound, then tears his shirt and presses it around his leg. Dark clouds scud by the summit. Above him the palm trees are whipping in the wind. The ocean is black and angry. Huge waves crash on the reef.

EXT. CHUCK'S CAMPSITE DAY MOMENTS LATER
Chuck struggles to cover the FedEx boxes with the remains of the raft. The wind is blowing hard now, tearing at the raft, so Chuck anchors it with rocks. The first drops of rain pelt his face.

EXT. LIMPET POINT DAY MOMENTS LATER

As the rain comes down and the waves build, Chuck limps through the shallows, then up the rocks toward the cave, seeking shelter from the storm.

EXT. LOWER CAVE DARK GREY GLOOMY DAY MOMENTS LATER

Chuck crawls through the mouth of the cave.

INT. LOWER CAVE DARK GREY GLOOMY DAY MOMENTS LATER

Using Al's mag light to see, he enters the cave, then drags himself onto a rock by the entrance. He collapses on the floor. He clicks his mag light off.

EXT. CAVE ENTRANCE NIGHT LATER

Lightning and rain batter the cave. Surf surges into the cave entrance, lapping at where Chuck lies huddled on the rock and waking him up. He shines the light onto the water. It's too deep to wade out now. He's trapped. He could die here.

Shining the light farther into the cave, he sees a narrow passage leading up. Like a wounded animal, Chuck painfully, slowly, climbs to safety.

INT. UPPER CAVE NIGHT MOMENTS LATER

Chuck emerges into the UPPER CAVE, a bigger cavern above the ocean. Precariously perched by the entrance, a palm tree whips and sways in the storm. Exhausted, Chuck leans back and closes his eyes, muttering in pain.

CHUCK

God... Oh God...

He sets the light on the ledge. Shaking and chilled, Chuck examines his wound. The gash in his leg is deep and jagged. It oozes blood. But there's nothing Chuck can do about it.

Chuck lies on his side in a pool of yellowish mud, lapping at the dripping rain water. Then he passes out.

The light slowly dies, leaving the cave in black.

EXT. CHUCK'S CAMPSITE DAY

The wind and rain batter Chuck's campsite. The tide is higher than we've ever seen it.

EXT. CAVE DAY

The rain has stopped. The sun breaks through beautiful white clouds.

INT. UPPER CAVE DAY

The palm tree blows lazily in the wind.

INT. UPPER CAVE DAY SAME

Chuck lies sleeping in semi-darkness. A point of sunlight streams through a crack in the wall of the cave and shines on his face. The point of light slowly moves toward his eyes.

The sunlight hits Chuck's eye. Blinking, he comes awake.

He picks up the mag light and clicks it on and off. The batteries are dead. He peels away the blood-caked bandage from his wound, which is scabbed and healing.

Remembering the watch, he checks his pocket. What a relief: it's still there.

He starts to crawl back down the narrow passage.

EXT. CHUCK'S CAMPSITE LATER THAT DAY

Swaying, his weight still on his good leg, Chuck considers the remains of his camp. The boxes are clustered under the raft, which has been swept against some palm trees. He knows now he's imprisoned on this island. The rescuers aren't going to find him. His escape attempt was an utter failure. So he better survive.

Chuck gets down on his hands and knees and slurps some water that's collected in the folds of the raft. Sphew! It's salty and stagnant! He spits it out.

Still weak, he fumbles through the coconuts, finds one that's been opened. Holding it to his mouth, he sucks out the last sips of milk. Then he looks at the FedEx boxes.

EXT. CHUCK'S CAMPSITE LATER THAT DAY

Rip! Chuck tears open one of the boxes. Out tumble some VIDEO-TAPES labeled in Japanese. Chuck looks at them: what good are they?

He opens another box covered with Post-Its and sheathed in blue. A divorce decree.

He opens another box that contains a gaily wrapped package, inside of which is a WILSON VOLLEYBALL and a birthday card. He reads the card.

                                    CHUCK
    "The most beautiful thing in the world is of course the world itself. Johnny, have the happiest birthday ever. Love, your Grandpa."

He sets the card aside. He unwraps the volleyball, then sets it aside. No time for play now.

He picks up the Angel Wing Box and stares at the drawing. It's so strange to see such an evocative piece of art on a box, here, on this island. Someone cared a lot, went to a lot of trouble. Chuck looks at the label, reads who it's from. There's something about those wings. He sets that box aside, unopened.

He opens the next-to-last box. Inside is a pair of child's ICE SKATES with white boots wrapped in bubble wrap. Ice skates. Great.

He opens the last box, which contains a DESIGNER DRESS. He holds it up. Imagine the woman inside it. No, can't go there.

EXT. CAMPSITE DAY LATER
Using an ice skate, Chuck cuts a piece of fabric from the remainder of his pant leg to make a new bandage, covers it in bubble wrap, and then binds it to his leg with laces from the other skate.

EXT. CAMPSITE DAY LATER
Chuck stretches the raft over a log frame to make a tent. He spreads the unfolded FedEx boxes out, making himself a soft bed.

EXT. CAMPSITE DAY LATER
Thonk! Chuck opens a coconut with the spike on the end of the skate blade. Thonk, he does another, then another. So easy with the right tool.

EXT. BEACH DAY LATER
Chuck has rigged a fishing net made from the dress that he found in

one of the FedEx boxes. He catches a sardine and eats it raw.

EXT. CAMPSITE DAY LATER
Chuck sharpens a stick with the blade of the skates.

EXT. LAGOON DAY
Chuck resumes his fishing. A shape scuttles raggedly beneath him. A crab. He freezes, holding his spear motionless.
The crab scurries into some rocks. Chuck stares into the rocks, then stabs down with his spear. He carefully lifts out the spear. On the end is the crab.
He twists off a claw, expecting to see flaky white meat. But a crab has an exoskeleton. The flesh simply pours out; it's more repulsive than mucous. No way he could eat that.
This is too much. Something's got to change. Something's got to be done, that crucial first step of civilization, from raw to cooked.

EXT. CHUCK'S CAMPSITE LATER THAT DAY
Chuck tries to spin a pointed stick into a wide flat piece of driftwood. Some shredded paper and small twigs lie on the flat stick, ready to be fed into the fire.

EXT. CHUCK'S CAMPSITE LATE DAY
Chuck keeps on trying to spin the stick. His hands are blistered and bloody.

EXT. CHUCK'S CAMPSITE DUSK
Kachink! We see a spark fly. Chuck is trying to start a fire by striking sparks off the ice skates. Ka-chink! Another spark flies! But each ember dies before it gets to the tinder.

EXT. CHUCK'S CAMPSITE NIGHT LATER
Chuck goes back to spinning the stick between his hands.

EXT. CAMPSITE NEXT DAY
His hands bandaged with strips of his T-shirt, Chuck saws with a stick, rubbing it back and forth on another stick he's wedged between two rocks.

Chuck stops, breathing hard. Then he tries to urge himself on.

                          CHUCK
          Come on!

He starts again. Sweat pours off his face. He's worn a groove into the
larger stick, but nothing's happened. It's hopeless. But he won't stop,
he's beyond reason. Suddenly the stick he's sawing with breaks!
It jabs into his already raw hands, tearing the blisters!

                          CHUCK (cont'd)
          Goddammittt!

Rage comes over him, total rage, fury at what has happened, at fate,
at himself. He screams, then screams again and throws the stick as far
as he can.
He picks up the larger grooved stick and SMASHES it against a palm
tree! The stick fractures! Chuck flings it away, then kicks the FedEx
boxes, scattering everything. He grabs the volleyball and, with a cry
of rage, flings it away. Finally he sinks down into the sand and puts
his head in his bloody hands.

EXT. BEACH DAY HALF HOUR LATER
Chuck rinses his hands in the still waters of the lagoon.

EXT. CAMPSITE DAY LATER
Chuck's hands are rebandaged; he's eating coconut meat listlessly.
The ball is there beside him. He reaches down and picks it up. His
bloody smudged HANDPRINT is on it.
For a long moment he stares at the ball. Then he licks one of his fingers and draws a mouth on the ball. Licking his fingers again, he
draws eyes.

                          CHUCK
          So –
He glances at the label.

CHUCK (cont'd)

Wilson.

Chuck sets Wilson down on a log overlooking the fire-making.

CHUCK (cont'd)

One more time. That's it. One more.

Chuck walks over and picks up the broken stick, which has a perpendicular crack at the groove, leaving an open space beneath the groove. He saws away, sweating, working harder and harder. Nothing happens. He keeps on, but then he senses Wilson's presence. Continuing to saw on the fire stick, he glances over at Wilson.

CHUCK (cont'd)

You wouldn't have a match, would you, pal?

No, Wilson doesn't have a match. Chuck keeps sawing.

EXT. CAMPSITE DAY LATER

Close on sawing stick. Sweat falls on it from Chuck's face. A trickle of blood runs out of the bandage on Chuck's hands.
Suddenly a wisp of smoke curls out from the groove!

EXT. CAMPSITE DAY SAME

Chuck glances over at Wilson – can you believe this? – and saws with all his strength.
The smoke increases. He picks up his stick and stares at –

ECU EMBER

The tiny glowing spark that glows in the blackened groove.

EXT. CAMPSITE DAY SAME

Chuck blows gently on the spark, so gently, the breath of life.

ECU EMBER

The golden red glow slowly dies into black. It's dead. Chuck stares at it in despair, then over to Wilson.

CHUCK

The air! The air got to it!

EXT. CAMPSITE DAY SAME

Chuck stares at the dead ember, then he realizes: he knows, he knows how to do it!

EXT. CAMPSITE DAY LATER

Chuck shreds a nest of coconut fiber into a ball and gently places it under the groove in his stick.

EXT. CAMPSITE DAY LATER

The sun is going down. Chuck is still sawing. Again the smoke appears. Sweating, he saws frantically.

Chuck tears away the saw stick, picks up the nest of tinder, and blows on it gently. The smoke increases. He blows some more. Another fragile crimson spark appears.

CHUCK

Careful now, careful...

ECU EMBER

The ember fades, almost dies, then glows and glows brighter, then as Chuck blows on it the ember spreads to the coconut fiber.

EXT. CAMPSITE DAY SAME

Chuck gently places the tinder in the paper, then blows on it as if he were holding life itself. Suddenly a tiny tongue of flame flickers and catches!

CHUCK

Fire!

He feeds in more paper, more twigs. The flames lick out, catch, grow.

CHUCK (cont'd)

Wilson! Fire!

EXT. CHUCK'S CAMPSITE MAGIC HOUR LATER

Chuck rushes about, piling on driftwood, exultant in the firelight. He sings at the top of his lungs. Come on baby light my fire! He beats a log with sticks and dances in the firelight. The time to hesitate is through! Chuck drags another log toward the fire. No time to wallow in the mire!

He tosses it on. Try to set the night on fire-uh!

Then he stands back and regards what he has created.

                         CHUCK
     Fire. I have created... fire.

Chuck grabs a palm frond and waves it, sending sparks flying up into the sky. They climb and sparkle until they merge with the stars.

EXT. CHUCK'S CAMPSITE NIGHT LATER

Skewered on a stick, a crab cooks in the fire, which now roars, fueled by stacks of driftwood. Chuck can't wait to eat it. He takes the crab off the stick, burning his fingers, but he doesn't care. Breaking open the claw, he pulls out the steaming, perfectly cooked meat, then gently puts it into his mouth. Sure, his tooth hurts a little, but who cares?

EXT. CHUCK'S CAMPSITE STILL LATER THAT NIGHT

We find a big pile of crab shells and beside them, Chuck sated as he finishes his last crab, wincing slightly from the pain in his tooth.

                         CHUCK
(to Wilson)
          Tomorrow, Wilson. We'll go make a signal fire. Up at the sum-
          mit. So ships can see. They'll see. We're getting out of here.

EXT. SUMMIT DAY LATER

Chuck has rigged a ramp of logs and rocks, onto which he has fire-wood so that as each log burns, another one slides down into a sig-nal fire. Once the fire is going, he stands up and looks to all the points of the compass. But the sky and the sea are empty.

EXT. CAMPSITE DAY LATER

Chuck carves a mark in a palm tree. It's a calendar. A small fire at the campsite smolders. In the b.g. on the summit we can see smoke from the signal fire.

He starts to count the marks. There are twelve marks.

Boom. We hear the roar of thunder. Chuck looks up at the sky. Here come those dark clouds again. The first raindrops hit him.

EXT. CAMPSITE DAY MOMENTS LATER

Rain lands hissing in the fire. Chuck tries to cover the fire with the remains of the raft, but the wind blows it away. The rain comes down harder! Steam pours out of the fire, red gives way to dead black. Without shelter, his fire is useless.

INT. CAVE DAY LATER

Chuck enters carrying the coconut shell, in which burns a sheet of paper from the divorce settlement. He is carrying a bundle of wood and twigs wrapped in his sweater. He fans the flames in the coconut shell, keeping the fire alive.

INT. CAVE GREY DAY RAIN

We start on Wilson's enigmatic face flickering in the firelight.

Shadows thrown up by the firelight dance on the walls of the cave. A full fire burns now.

Outside the rain comes down in torrents.

Chuck is drawing the path of the doomed plane on the cave wall with a charred stick as he explains his calculations to Wilson.

> CHUCK
>
> Out of radio contact an hour, maybe more, flying around that storm, so they think we were here, but really we were here – say, 400 miles off course.

He starts to figure the area of a circle with a radius of 400 miles.

> CHUCK (cont'd)
> Circle, radius 400, squared, times pi, that's...

(holy shit)

... 500,000 square miles. That's twice the size of Texas.
(beat)

They may never find us.

The last tiny flames of fire flicker away. Chuck slowly makes his way to the dying fire and gently blows at the embers, which brings it back to life. He feeds new twigs to the flickering flames. His hands slips into the soft yellow mud. Chuck looks at his hand which is now covered in yellow mud. Chuck presses his hand on the wall of the cave, leaving his hand print. He steps back and regards the hand. In the firelight it almost seems to be waving at him.

CHUCK (cont'd)

Chuck was here.

Wilson gives that same enigmatic smile.

EXT. LAGOON DAY
Chuck pulls some mollusks off the rocks. Above him, on the summit, we can see smoke from the fire.

EXT. LAGOON DAY
Chuck gathers different colored seashells.

EXT. JUNGLE DAY
Chuck collects red clay in a seashell.

INT. CAVE DAY
Chuck has made three more hand prints on the wall next to the muddy one from before. The new hand prints are made from his new colors.
Chuck grinds seashells with a rock mortar into a rock bowl, making a reddish paste out of clay. Next to him are seashells holding four other colors: white, yellow, brownish-orange, and black.
He glances down at the Angel Wing Box. The wings seem to be flying. It's like magic.

He makes a few tentative marks on the wall, trying to draw a wing.

EXT. CAMPSITE DAY LATER
Chuck makes another mark on the calendar tree. There are over
twenty now.
Around one he has drawn a red flame the day he got fire. Another
has a gray tombstone Al. Yet another has four bars of color – the
day he began to make art.

INT. CAVE NIGHT
From Wilson we go to the cave wall, past crude finger drawings of
spirals and suns, then on to wings, wings after wings, in different colors, but finally trying to match the ones on the box.
We find the watch with Kelly's picture in it propped up on a rock,
and then we come to Chuck, who works on a portrait of Kelly using
his new paints and a brush made of a frayed root. He makes another
mark on the face, then steps back and turns to Wilson.

                                CHUCK
            She's better-looking in real life, believe me.

Chuck stares at the painting, then at the photograph. He's completely, utterly alone. Lost. Cut off from everything he ever had or
ever knew. All he has are memories and a volleyball.

EXT. CHUCK'S CAMPSITE DAY
In the shiny surface of the ice skates the reflection of Chuck's face
comes into view. He stares at the mouth, trying to finger the sore tooth.

EXT. CAMPSITE DAY LATER
Chuck mixes a mash of mud and seawater. He tries to pack his sore
tooth with it, but it's so sensitive even this hurts now.

                                CHUCK
(to Wilson)
            Want to hear something funny? Back home, in Memphis, my
            dentist's name is Doctor Spalding.

97

He tries to grin, but his tooth just hurts too much.

EXT. LAGOON DAY
Chuck tries to fill his mouth with sea water. The pain is so great his
eyes water.

INT. UPPER CAVE DAY LATER
Chuck tears a dress into strips, soaks the strips in sea water, then lays
them out, ready to use.
Using one of the ice skate blades propped as a mirror, Chuck picks up
the other ice skate. He opens his mouth wide, positions the sharp end
of the skate blade in back of the tooth and picks up a round stone.

                              CHUCK
          One, two...

He brings the hammer stone down hard on the skate blade! The tooth
shoots out toward the camera! Chuck SCREAMS and falls to the
ground. He BLACKS OUT and so does the screen.

FADE IN:

EXT. LAGOON FISH DAY
A fish swims in the clear water. Suddenly, Ka – swoosh!! A sharpened
stick shoots through it, sending a cloud of blood into the water.
We TILT UP out of the water to Chuck – a stunning contrast to how
we last saw him. Now he is gaunt, scarred, brown as a berry. A few
untended sores mark his body. His ordeal has burned the fat off both
his body and his soul. He barely glances at the fish on the end of the
spear. His eyes are bottomless. On screen see: FOUR YEARS LATER.

EXT. LAGOON DAY

Carrying the fish, Chuck walks mechanically across the coral and the rocks barefoot. He doesn't even feel them anymore. He doesn't feel much of anything.

EXT. BEACH DAY

He walks past the old calendar tree, which is covered with marks. Next to it are two other trees, also covered. Chuck doesn't even notice.

He walks by the RUINS OF A CAMP, what looks to have once been a carefully made compound is now deteriorated and decaying back into the jungle. We see the gray dead remnants of a fire pit ringed with shells.

Chuck sinks to the ground. He doesn't really care where he sits. He faces away from the ocean. He never even looks out there anymore. Picking up a shard of rock, he cuts at the fish. Not even bothering to cook it, he sticks a piece of raw flesh into his mouth and chews it, a remote expression on his face. He is alive, but that's all he is. He's lost all hope.

EXT. BEACH DAY WIDE

Chuck lies asleep in the dirt, his back to the ocean.

EXT. BEACH DAY CHUCK'S FACE LATER

Rain pours down on Chuck's face as he sleeps. He doesn't even care. He comes slowly awake and licks a few drops as they stream down his face, as any simple living organism would do: to survive.

We WIDEN as the rain falls harder and the wind begins to blow, whipping the palm trees. It's a storm now. Chuck picks up what's left of the fish and slowly walks through the rain.

INT. CAVE DAY MOMENTS LATER

As the storm rages outside, Chuck climbs up into the cave carrying what's left of the fish. We see his old paintings and, beyond them, new ones. They deteriorate into dark spirals and primitive images, the final ones scratched out. We see broken shells crusted with dried paint, some old root brushes, all long abandoned.

The Angel Wing Box is cast into a corner. Stuffed with grass, Wilson sits in a pile of garbage, surrounded by discarded coconut husks, his face faded. There's an ellipse calendar Chuck long ago puzzled out on the cave wall. He ignores it and lies down to sleep, his face in the mud.

INT. CAVE DAY LATER

Chuck sleeps in the same spot. Suddenly we hear a noise. Thonk-thonk, thonk-thonk. His eyes come open in sudden fear. What was that? Was he hallucinating? Dreaming? He hasn't heard that sort of man-made sound in four years.

Trembling, he goes to the cave opening and listens, but there's nothing, only the sounds of the wind and surf and the dark clouds in the sky.

He sits down in the mud and idly puts the remains of the fish to his mouth, tearing at its guts, sucking the juices out of its skull. It's all just fuel to him.

And then, for no apparent reason, as he chews he begins to cry. Tears stream down his face. He takes another bite of the raw fish and continues to cry.

INT. CAVE NIGHT

Thunder crashes. Lightning flashes outside, revealing Chuck asleep again in the dark cave. The fires are out.

INT. CAVE DAY

Chuck sleeps on the floor of the cave. Sleeping is all he does, day and night. Suddenly there's that sound again. Thonk-thonk, thonk-thonk. He comes awake. Dammit!! He yells at Wilson.

                    CHUCK
    Shut up!

He stares hard at Wilson's faded face.

                 CHUCK (cont'd)
        A little sleep!!! That's all I want!

He lies back down and closes his eyes. Thonk-thonk. Thonk-thonk.

That damn sound again.

CHUCK (cont'd)

    Dammit!!

Chuck goes to the cave opening. The storm is over. Thonk-thonk, thonk-thonk. But he can't see anything, only the dark blue ocean and the empty sky.

EXT. CAVE POINT LATER THAT DAY
Carrying his spear, Chuck wades around the corner of Cave Point. Beyond him we see the cave opening and the palm tree. THONK-THONK. THONK-THONK.

EXT. CAVE POINT DAY MOMENTS LATER
Chuck stops and stares and we see what he sees.

HIS VIEW PORTAPOTTY
It's a PortaPotty, or half of one. Banging gently against the rocks. Thonk-thonk, thonk-thonk.

EXT. CAVE POINT ON CHUCK SAME
His synapses take a long time to fire, the connections are like taffy. But then what he sees begins to sink in.
With his stick he pokes at it. It bobs a little. He tries to lift it up. Too heavy. He knocks off a piece of seaweed, revealing lettering that reads Bakersfi –

CHUCK

    Bakersfield.

EXT. CAVE ENTRANCE DAY LATER
Wilson sits on a little pile of sand, facing the PortaPotty. Chuck crouches beside him, staring at the PortaPotty, which Chuck has erected on the sand.

EXT. CAVE ENTRANCE SUNSET
Still staring at the PortaPotty, Chuck's now on the opposite side of it.

Sand drips through his fingers. Suddenly the breeze blows the PortaPotty over, settling it gently in the sand. That makes Chuck start; the sand stops dribbling through his fingers.

EXT. CAVE ENTRANCE NIGHT
Lost in thought, Chuck paces around the fallen PortaPotty.

EXT. CAVE ENTRANCE NEXT DAY
Chuck's shadow falls across the PortaPotty. We PULL BACK to reveal him standing right over it. He's figured something out. He looks over at Wilson, then out at the reef where the waves are breaking.

                    CHUCK
        This could work.
(beat)
        This could work.

The light is coming back into his eyes.

EXT. AL'S ROCK MAGIC HOUR
Whoosh! A burning palm tree falls into frame as two others burn beside it. PAN to Chuck hacking at the burnt-off base with his ice skate.

EXT. CHUCK'S CAMP DAY LATER
Rip! He tears palm fronds off one of the collapsed lean-to's, revealing a framework of driftwood.

EXT. CHUCK'S CAMP DAY LATER
He lays poles of driftwood across the frame, mumbling a count to himself as he goes.

                    CHUCK
    … .fifty-two, fifty-three lashings.

He turns to Wilson.

CHUCK (cont'd)

We're going to have to make rope again.

He considers the frame and all the poles across it.

CHUCK (cont'd)

A whole lot of rope.

There's an edge in his voice, as if the act of making rope brings back unpleasant memories.

EXT. JUNGLE DAY ECU
Chop! The ice skate ax hacks down a sapling. Chop! Another. Chop! And another.

EXT. AL'S ROCK DAY LATER
Chuck dumps a load of cut saplings at Al's rock. Rip! He skins the bark off one, throws it in a pile of skinned bark. Rip! Skins another one and tosses it in the same pile. The skinned saplings land in another pile.

EXT. AL'S ROCK NIGHT
He's weaving the skinned bark into cords.

CHUCK

... .fifty-three lashings, say twenty feet per lashing...

INT. CAVE DAY
Now he's weaving those cords into ropes.

CHUCK

... that's a thousand sixty feet of rope...

He stops, measures the rope he's just made against his arm, does some figures in his head.

CHUCK (cont'd)
… .I'm doing forty feet a day…

He looks over at the ellipse calendar, which is marked with symbols showing tide and moon phases and wind that Chuck observed over the years. A dot of sunlight falls on it.

CHUCK (cont'd)
… that's, what? twenty-six days…
He moves his hand from the dot of light hitting the calendar, tracking the days, figuring everything out.

CHUCK (cont'd)
… which should put us here…

He makes a mark on the calendar.

CHUCK (cont'd)
Right when the tides are the highest. When we've got the best shot at an offshore wind.

He thinks about all he's got to do.

CHUCK (cont'd)
It's going to be tight. Even if we use videotape for the deck lashings.

Determined, he starts weaving more rope. He's back in FedEx deadline mode, but this time with a heavy dose of irony.

CHUCK (cont'd)
TIME, WILSON, WE LIVE OR DIE BY IT. WE CAN NEVER COMMIT THE sin… of turning our back on time.

EXT. LAGOON DAY
Chuck pushes the logs through the lagoon toward Rocky Point.

EXT. ROCKY POINT DAY

Using the rope we saw him make, Chuck lashes the first big pontoon to the driftwood frame, which sits perched on the palm logs, one side extended out over the water.

EXT. ROCKY POINT DAY

Chuck dumps a load of driftwood poles down by the raft frame.

EXT. ROCKY POINT DAY

Chuck pulls videotape out of one of his cassettes and uses it to lash down a driftwood pole, making a deck.

EXT. ROCKY POINT DAY

He struggles to lift another big pontoon into place, on the side of the raft nearest the water.

EXT. ROCKY POINT DAY

He's lashing the last pontoon now, pulling up rope as he goes. Suddenly he's at the end. There's no more. And he's way short.

EXT. AL'S ROCK DAY

Chuck dumps a couple of saplings down on the ground. Wilson sits on the log.

                    CHUCK
          That's the last of them.
(beat)
          I've been over the whole damn island. This is all there is.
(beat)
          I know what you're thinking. We know where thirty feet of
          rope is. Forget it. You know what happened the last time. I'm
          never going back up there.

Then he looks down at the saplings.

                    CHUCK (cont'd)
          I'll just use videotape. It'll work.

He hesitates for a moment, then gets really mad at Wilson.

                    CHUCK (cont'd)
        It'll work, dammit!! Come on!

EXT. ROCKY POINT DAY
Chuck finishes lashing down that last pontoon joint with videotape.
He makes an emphatic big knot. Done. Then he turns to Wilson.

                    CHUCK
        See?

He heads over to the other side and cinches down that knot, which is
made of the bark rope. As he does – POP! – the videotape lashing on
the other side breaks. The pontoon shifts free. Chuck stares at it, then
at Wilson, then up at the summit.

                    CHUCK (cont'd)
        Not a word. Don't say a word.

INT. CAVE DAY
He tosses Wilson unceremoniously on the floor of the cave, then
searches through the videotape cassettes, tossing aside the empty ones.
He finds a full cassette, tries to pull out the tape, but he's so impatient
that he gives up and smashes it with a rock.

                    CHUCK
        Just make a stronger weave, that's all.

He's trying to weave strands together, but it gets all tangled. Then he
gets a piece made.

                    CHUCK (cont'd)
        Told you. It's fine. Fine.

He pulls on it, testing it. It breaks. For a long moment he holds the
broken piece in his hand. Then he looks over at Wilson.

CHUCK (cont'd)
Okay. You win.

He gets up to leave, then turns to Wilson.

CHUCK (cont'd)
But if I don't come back, it's on your head.

EXT. SUMMIT SUNSET LATER THAT DAY
Carrying a long forked stick, Chuck climbs warily up to the top. He's almost shaking. It's like going back to the scene of a terrible accident. It's taking all his courage to do this.
The tree at the very top has been torn almost in half. One of the limbs has fallen over the side. He looks down over the side, then tries to poke something with the stick. No luck.
Mustering his courage, he climbs out onto the split tree, out over the edge. The waves crash on the rocks far below. This is really scary.
Balancing as well as he can, he reaches down with the stick, feels for something, concentrates – ahhh!!! – grabs it. Gingerly he edges back down the tree, trying not to lose whatever he's hooked on the end of the stick.
Safely back on solid ground, he pulls in the stick. Hooked onto it is a thick woven rope.
Chuck begins to pull it up, foot after foot of thick rope. It's hard to do. Something's on the end. Finally whatever it is comes up over the edge, and then we see it: a heavy log totem, strikingly human-like, two trunks for arms, a face painted on.
Around its neck is – a hangman's noose.
Chuck stares at it. That could have been him on the end of the rope. Then he undoes the noose.
He stands the totem up, then turns it to face the setting sun.

INT. CAVE NIGHT
Chuck tosses the rope down in front of Wilson, who sits by the smoldering fire. There's the noose, eloquent evidence of how desperate and deep was Chuck's despair. He looks over at Wilson, whose face seems smug.

                                CHUCK

You were right, it wouldn't have been a quick snap. I would
have landed on the rocks and bled to death. Might have taken
days. So what?

His back to Wilson, Chuck starts rekindling the fire. Suddenly he
whirls around, as if Wilson said something to really make him mad.

                          CHUCK (cont'd)

I said so what!

(beat)

Well let me tell you something. Between this shithole and the
ocean, I'd sure rather die out there!

He's getting madder and madder.

                          CHUCK (cont'd)

We finally get a chance to get out of here, and you're pissing all
over it?! You're scared, that's all it is!! You're yellow!! Well
I'm sick of it! Sick of it!

He picks up Wilson and screams right into his face.

                          CHUCK (cont'd)

I'm not spending the rest of my life talking to a damn volleyball!

He kicks Wilson as hard as he can! Bam, boom, Wilson bounces off
the walls and then shoots out the palm tree cave opening!! He's gone.
For a brief moment there's a smile on Chuck's face. He's finally got
rid of that damn ball.

                          CHUCK (cont'd)

That'll shut you up.

And then he realizes what he's done. Oh no. He scrambles to the cave
opening.

                    CHUCK (cont'd)
    Wilson!!!

EXT. CAVE OPENING NIGHT
Lit by the moonlight, Chuck scrambles out into the rocks.

                              CHUCK
    Wilson!!!

Desperate, Chuck searches for Wilson.

EXT. CAVE POINT NIGHT
Chuck splashes out into the water.

                              CHUCK
    Wilson!!

EXT. CAVE POINT NIGHT
Chuck splashes around the rocks, desperate.

                              CHUCK
    Wilson, I'm sorry. Come back.

Suddenly, the moonlight catches a flash of white on top of a gentle
wave.

                         CHUCK (cont'd)
    Wilson!!

He half swims, half runs toward it.

EXT. AL'S ROCK LATER THAT NIGHT
Chuck's got a big fire going. He holds up Wilson, looking at him with
great affection. A big chunk of paint was torn off Wilson's face when
Chuck kicked him.
Chuck takes a stone knife and draws it across his knuckles. The blood
starts to flow. With his own blood he repairs Wilson's face.

                        CHUCK
    There. There. That's my old pal.

He holds Wilson up to examine him, the fresh blood glistening in the
firelight.

                        CHUCK (cont'd)
    Okay? You okay?

EXT. ROCKY POINT DAY
CHUCK TIES A WINDSOCK MADE OF A STRIP OF THE OLD DRESS TO A
STICK AND THEN WE PULL BACK TO REVEAL THE ENTIRE FINISHED RAFT,
PERCHED ATOP THE BIG PALM LOGS LEADING DOWN TO THE WATER. IT'S
ALL LASHED TOGETHER. THE PortaPotty sits on top of the deck like a
tent.

INT. CAVE DAY
Chuck fills up the life-raft bag with tools. He glances over at the
ellipse. The light has reached the mark Chuck made to designate his
departure date. Then he picks up the Angel Wing Box. Should he take
it? He decides against it, sets it back down, and heads out.
After a beat, he comes back and picks up the Angel Wing Box. It's
coming with him.

EXT. ROCKY POINT DAY
The wind sock blows gently as Chuck wraps the Angel Wing Box
with old bubble wrap and yellow life-raft material. Stacks of coconuts
are already on the raft, as are fishing lines, spears, the life-raft bag full
of tools.

EXT./INT. RAFT MOMENTS LATER
Holding the Angel Wing Box, Chuck crawls under the PortaPotty
shelter and starts to lash it to the decking. As he works, he glances up
at the PortaPotty above him and gets an idea.

EXT. ROCKY POINT DAY
Lying on his back under the PortaPotty like Michelangelo in the

Sistine Chapel, Chuck works with his paints on the inside of the PortaPotty. We can't see what he's doing. Above him the sky is darkening. The wind sock rustles this way, then that.

Chuck slips out from under the PortaPotty to take a look at the windsock. It blows out to sea for a moment, then flutters and dies. Chuck goes back to work.

EXT. AL'S ROCK NIGHT

By the firelight Chuck is trying to get some sleep. Al's grave looms right behind him. He looks over at Wilson.

> CHUCK
> What's the matter? Can't sleep?

He glances over at Al's grave, then picks up Wilson.

> CHUCK (cont'd)
> You're scared, aren't you?

He lies down and cradles Wilson in his arms.

> CHUCK (cont'd)
> That's okay. We're all scared.

Chuck has finally learned to be simple, honest, and direct, even if it's only to a volleyball. He closes his eyes. We linger on the two of them, together in the firelight, with Al's rock behind them.

EXT. AL'S ROCK EARLY THE NEXT MORNING

Chuck carves on Al's Rock with the worn-down ice skate. He's written: "Chuck Noland lvd here 1500 days alone, then tr'd escpe. Tell Kelly Frears in Mmphs Tn – " Chuck says the last words as he writes them.

> CHUCK
> "Chuck loved her."

He's carving the "h," then the "e" of "her." Then the wind whistles up around him. He stops and looks up at another windsock he's stuck on a stick by Al's rock. The sock rustles, then blows out to sea. Chuck drops the ice skate.

CHUCK (cont'd)
Wilson! High tide! Offshore breeze! Crunch time!

INT. CHUCK'S CAVE DAY MOMENTS LATER
Chuck bursts in, gathering up his last items as the wind begins to howl outside. He sees the watch with Kelly's photo. He thinks for a moment: can't leave that. Taking the cord holding his tooth off his neck, he strings the watch on it, then puts the watch around his neck, like a talisman.

He takes one last look around the cave – at all the paintings, the calendar, all the evidence of the years he spent here, all the loneliness, all those days and nights he had to fill. Goodbye to all that.

EXT. ROCKY POINT LATER THAT MORNING
Chuck's taken the pole the windsock was on to use as a lever to crank the raft off its perch on the two palm logs.

CHUCK
Crunch... time.

Unhhh!! The raft moves. He levers it some more, then shoves it. Now gravity takes over. The raft slides down the logs and – SPLASH!! – floats triumphantly in the lagoon.

EXT. LAGOON DAY
Chuck finishes tying Wilson securely onto his perch, facing forward like a figurehead. He looks past Wilson at the waves breaking on the reef.

CHUCK
This is it. I'll do it all. All you have to do is hang on.

EXT. LAGOON DAY

Splash, the videotape oars hit the water. We PAN UP to Chuck, who keeps his eye on the big waves over his shoulder as he rows out toward the reef.

Boom! He rows through the first breaker. Boom! He rows through another, struggling to keep from capsizing.

Then he's through! But up ahead, here comes one of those huge waves! The storm winds ruffle the crest, but the huge wave powers forward with incredible force.

For a moment Chuck is struck with terror. What was he thinking, to think he could beat this?

                              CHUCK
          Not yet... not yet... now!!

Then he commits. Totally. He ships the oars! He bends down, jerks on a slip knot that ties one end of the PortaPotty to the deck, then kicks it into the air. The wind catches it, and UP GOES THE PORTA-POTTY!

It's a SAIL! On it Chuck has painted the ANGEL WINGS. The wave is almost on him! WHOOMPH! The big sail catches the wind! Chuck struggles to hold the ropes that keep it trimmed into the wind. WHAM! The raft shoots forward! Chuck hangs on for dear life!

The raft powers right at the huge oncoming wave! BOOM! The wave rolls down. The raft disappears! Then, suddenly, it shoots out the other side!

Chuck's out! He can't believe it! But there's no time to celebrate. Here comes another roller! Powered by the wind, the raft goes up and over. The wave breaks behind him!

Chuck struggles to drop the sail as the raft swings around in the wind! He throws the sea anchor behind the raft!

The raft slides down the side of a huge wave! But the sea anchor holds!

                              CHUCK (cont'd)
          We did it! Wilson! We did it!

EXT. OCEAN SUNSET
Chuck turns Wilson around so he can see where they came from.

HIS VIEW ISLAND
We see the island silhouetted against the sky, tiny in the vast ocean
surrounding it.

EXT. OCEAN SUNSET
Chuck stares at it for a long time as a small squall sweeps over it,
obscuring the island in clouds. A rainbow forms where the island had
been. The raft drifts toward the setting sun.

EXT. OCEAN DAYS LATER
In the f.g. we see Wilson, tied to the mast. One of the ropes that
lashes him has started to decay. We PAN 360 around him to the vast
empty ocean on every side. We hear the rhythmic sound of oars hitting the water.
When we return to Wilson we see Chuck rowing mechanically. The
PortaPotty is up to catch the faint breeze. Chuck's sunburned and
marked with sores. He's wrapped a kind of headdress over his head
to protect his eyes.
The raft has deteriorated. Some lashings have come undone. All but a
few of the coconuts are gone. Strips of drying fish and fish bones lie
cast around.

EXT. OCEAN NIGHT
Chuck rows at night, PortaPotty sail still up. As he rows he looks up
at the stars burning furiously. He sees something else – a moving,
blinking light. An airplane.

                                 CHUCK
      Where do you think that one's headed? Tahiti? Fiji? Maybe it's
      the Sydney sweep.

The one he was on, so many years ago.

EXT. OCEAN DAY

A paddle hits the water. Then again, slow, barely moving. We MOVE
UP the oar to find Chuck, so tired he's dozing at the oars. There's no
wind. The PortaPotty is down. Suddenly Chuck comes awake and
starts to paddle again. He's not giving up.

EXT. OCEAN NIGHT

On Wilson in the moonlight, the ropes holding him fraying even
more. Chuck rows with what little strength he has, one stroke, then
another.
Suddenly we hear eerie music. A WHALE breaches, then dives, showing
its flukes in the moonlight. It breaches again. Its eye regards Chuck
for a long moment, then slides beneath the waves.

                              CHUCK
          Wilson, did you see that?

Chuck stares for a long moment at where the whale had been, then
starts to row again.

EXT. OCEAN DAY

It's raining, a steady monsoon rain. The water runs off the PortaPotty
and into a collection trough Chuck's rigged up, then into a coconut
canteen he holds beneath the stream.

EXT. OCEAN DAY

The rain has stopped. We PAN ACROSS the raft, but there's nothing
there. No Chuck. He's vanished.
Suddenly a spear breaks the water, with a fish on the end, followed by
Chuck, who's holding on to his life rope, which is made from the
rope he was going to use to hang himself. Out of breath, weak, he's
barely able to pull himself back to the raft.

EXT. OCEAN NIGHT

Wilson is in the f.g. The sky is dark, the sea angry. A big storm is
coming right at us across the ocean. CRACK! A bolt of lightning strikes
the ocean, sending a huge spout of water into the air. Chuck's hands

reach out, grab Wilson, and bring him onto the raft.

The storm hits just as Chuck pulls Wilson under the PortaPotty beneath the painted Angel Wings. The waves are huge, the wind tears at the raft, torrents of rain drive straight into Chuck's face.

Suddenly, WHOOSH! A blast of wind rips at the PortaPotty and tears it right off the raft!! The Angel Wings Chuck painted fly away, off into the storm.

EXT. OCEAN DAY

We start on Wilson, now barely tied on, gently tottering in what's left of his holder. The raft is all but destroyed. Not only is the PortaPotty gone, but so are a number of the deck poles. Chuck is asleep. The ocean is calm.

Suddenly Wilson teeters one last time, then falls off! He bounces against Chuck's foot, then into the ocean!

He floats slowly past the sleeping Chuck.

EXT. OCEAN WIDE

We see the raft, Chuck sleeping, and Wilson floating slowly away. Suddenly, WHOOSH! The whale breaches again, spouting.

EXT. RAFT SAME

A spray of water settles on Chuck as the whale's flukes splash back into the water. Chuck rolls over, looks around and sees Wilson's perch is empty.

> CHUCK
>
> Wilson?

Panicked, he struggles to his feet. He stares out at the ocean, looking, looking...

There! He sees the ball, floating gently away.

> CHUCK (cont'd)
>
> Wilson!

He plunges into the ocean, intent on rescuing Wilson. But he's so

weak he can hardly swim. Desperate, he grabs the life rope.
Hanging onto it with one hand, he stretches out to Wilson, but he
can't... quite... reach. Wilson floats away, just out of Chuck's grasp.
Wilson's barely above the water.
Chuck can let go of the rope and swim after Wilson, or he can hold
on to the raft. Decision time. Chuck desperately treads water. Waves
splash in his face, choking him.

CHUCK (cont'd)

Wilson!

Wilson floats farther away. Chuck lets go of the rope to swim after
him, but Wilson's sinking, sinking. He'll never get to him.
Suddenly Chuck's hand reaches out and grabs the rope, holding on
desperately. Barely able to tread water, he watches as Wilson slowly
sinks.

CHUCK (cont'd)

Wilson!

But he's gone. Only the waves remain.

EXT. RAFT SUNSET
Dripping wet, Chuck huddles on the raft, now utterly alone. He cries
big, deep sobs. Then he collapses onto the deck.
His hand falls on one of the oars. He picks it up, looks at it. What's the
point of this? He slowly lets the oar slide into the water, then does the
same with the other oar, watching as they slowly drift away. He's given
himself up to the ocean. Where it takes him, that's where he'll go.
The raft drifts away, getting smaller and smaller.

EXT. RAFT EXTREMELY HIGH ANGLE
The tiny raft drifts, a speck in the vast trackless ocean.

EXT. OCEAN UNDERWATER DAY
The raft is above us, a dark shadow against bright sunlight. We see
Chuck's hand motionless underwater, fingers just drifting. He might
be dead.

We see the water rippling through the frayed knots on the raft. In the water is a small fish, its eyes luminescent and curious. We see barnacles on the logs by Chuck's hand. We pick out the texture of the water-soaked wood.

EXT. RAFT DAY SAME
The sun is low. Then we hear that faint whale music. Suddenly spray floats over Chuck. And then more spray. Something nudges the raft, then Chuck's sprayed with more water. Chuck slowly rolls over. He opens his eyes.

CHUCK

Kelly? Kelly?

For a precious moment he thought they were together again. His eyes slowly close.
Passing right behind him, is the huge rusty hull of a big freighter. Suddenly he's sprayed again. The raft's nudged again. He lifts his head up, turns, and sees the ship.

EXT. OCEAN DAY SAME
And then we see the scene: in the b.g, the rusty freighter; then the ragged raft, with a weary Chuck rising up, reaching out to it; and, in the f.g., the flukes of a great whale as it dives back into the ocean.
It seems like the ship is going to go right past. He can't believe it, not after everything he's been through.
Then, suddenly, from the ship a FLARE shoots up. Its bells begin to sound. He's saved!

INT. HOUSE MEMPHIS DAY
A phone rings in the kitchen of a Chickasaw Gardens cottage. A hand picks it up. Kelly's hand.
She answers the phone. Her hair's short now.

KELLY

Hello?
(beat)
Oh, hi. How are you?

(beat, a little hesitant)
> Okay.

She listens, hearing news beyond belief. The man she was going to marry, the man she mourned and buried, the man she loved – is alive. The news sinks in, all those emotions play across her face.
Then she faints dead away, and as she sinks to the kitchen floor the camera moves around to reveal a LITTLE GIRL (1) sitting in a high chair and a MAN (JERRY) sitting at the breakfast table, his face changing as he leaps up to come to the aid of his – wife.

INT. FEDEX CHALLENGER APPROACHING MEMPHIS DAY
We start on a pair of running shoes, clean and brand new. We move up crisp new trousers to where a hand grips the armrest of a captain's chair, perhaps a bit too tightly, and another hand holds a glass of Dr Pepper with ice. There's a bottle of prescription pills on the armrest. We see a new shirt, and then, Chuck. He's clean-shaven, his hair is cut, but he's still thin and gaunt. On screen see: FOUR WEEKS LATER. In the b.g. Stan comes out of the cockpit toward us.

STAN
> Forty-five minutes.

(beat)
> You want another Dr Pepper?

CHUCK
> Sure. Do we have any ice left?

Stan pops another can at this little station where there's some drinks and ice.

STAN
> We've got plenty of ice. We've got ice out the kazoo.

He hands Chuck the drink. Chuck takes it, rattling the ice around absently.

STAN (cont'd)

Here's the drill. The plane pulls in, we get off, the ceremony'll be right there in the hangar. Fred Smith's going to say a few words; all you have to do is smile and wave and say thank you. Then we'll get you over to see Kelly.

CHUCK

What am I going to say? What do I say to her?

STAN

Whatever's in your heart, Chuck. There's no road map for this. You sure you want to do this?

Chuck nods. I want to. I think.

STAN (cont'd)

Kelly had to let you go. We all did. We buried you. We had a funeral, a coffin, the whole thing. It was tough. Real tough.

CHUCK

You had a coffin? What was in it?

STAN

We all put something in. A cell phone. A beeper. I put in an Elvis CD. Everything that was important to you.

The irony here goes unremarked. None of that is important to Chuck now.

CHUCK

So you had to go to two funerals.

Stan nods. Yeah.

CHUCK (cont'd)

I am so sorry I wasn't there when Mary died. You had to go

through all that without me. You needed me. I should have
been there.

Stan stares at him, at this direct, honest Chuck. So different now. And
his eyes say a simple wordless thanks.

INT. READY ROOM MEMPHIS
Kelly and Jerry stand in the Ready Room. Vending machines, pilot's
schedules, a few chairs, several TVs that show live the ceremony outside. Kelly is transfixed.

KELLY

Oh God, look at him. Look at him. Oh my God.

And what she sees is –

EXT. SUPERHUB PLATFORM DAY
A large crowd – band, media, hoopla – watches as Chuck stands next
to FRED SMITH, the chairman of FedEx, as he makes his welcome
speech.

FRED SMITH

Four years ago the FedEx family lost five of our sons. That was
a sad day, a tragic day. But today one of those sons, Chuck
Noland, has been returned to us. In the words of the gospel
hymn, he was lost, and now he's found. Like Lazarus, Chuck
has come back from the dead. So today, today is a joyful day.

We PULL BACK, away from the ceremony, as Fred Smith continues to
talk. Chuck keeps craning his neck, looking in their direction.

KELLY (O.S.)

What's he looking for? Haven't they told him? Doesn't he
know where we are?

And we keep pulling back, back into the ready room.

Kelly and Jerry watch the ceremony through the window and on the TV. Fred Smith's voice plays under throughout.

> JERRY
>
> They'll tell him. It's all set up.

Kelly stares at Chuck's image on the screen as if she were seeing a ghost. Jerry reaches over to take Kelly's hand. She's buffeted by all these conflicting emotions.

> FRED SMITH (ON TV)
>
> We at Federal Express know better than most that time waits for no man. But it can pause, just a moment, for us to honor one of our own. Chuck, this is your family, all of us. To our long-lost son. Welcome home.

The crowd cheers. Balloons rain down. On TV and through the window we see the ceremony end and Chuck leave, heading toward the Ready Room, escorted by Stan and pursued by reporters.

> KELLY
>
> Oh my God, here he comes. Look, he's walking so funny.

Chuck continues to approach, shedding reporters.
Through the window we see Chuck and Stan pause, Stan asking MOS if Chuck wants him to come with him. We see Chuck shake his head and then head right for us.

> KELLY (cont'd)
>
> Look at me. I'm shaking.

She holds out her hand. She can't control it.

> KELLY (cont'd)
>
> I'm scared to death.

JERRY

Of course you are. Anyone would be. But we'll get through it.

Kelly leans against a table.

KELLY

I should be standing up.

She quickly sits down.

KELLY (cont'd)
Sitting down. Sitting down.

But that's not right either. She stands back up.

KELLY (cont'd)
No. Here.

She turns and looks at Jerry.

KELLY (cont'd)
But you can't be here. I have to do it alone.

JERRY
We've been over this. We're doing it together.

KELLY
Please.

JERRY
You sure?

She nods, not sure of anything.
Jerry gives Kelly a hug of encouragement, then heads out the door,
leaving her standing there alone. She tugs at her clothes, brushes back
her hair, wets her lips.
Chuck's almost there.

EXT. READY ROOM MEMPHIS

Chuck stops at the door. He's nervous himself. He stops, turns, maybe he's the one who can't do it. Then he reaches into his pocket and pulls out the watch, the one Kelly had given him, the one with her picture. Okay.

INT. READY ROOM MEMPHIS

Watch in hand, Chuck enters – an empty room. He looks around. Takes the measure of the room. That's odd. Then the door opens. Chuck looks at it expectantly. And in comes... Jerry.

CHUCK

I must be in the wrong place. I was supposed to meet someone in Pilot Holding Lounge A.

JERRY

No. It's the right place. You probably don't remember me. I did a root canal on you. Al Spalding referred you.

CHUCK

Uh, yeah, yeah.

JERRY

I'M JERRY Lovett, Kelly's husband.

And now we're on Chuck as he struggles to hold in his emotions.

JERRY (cont'd)

Kelly wanted to talk to you, but – look, this is really hard. For everyone. I can't even imagine how hard it is for you. Kelly, she's really had it rough, too. When she thought you were dead, she didn't come out of her house for a year. Now, dealing with all this... It's real confusing. Real emotional. Just give her some time. A little time.

As Jerry talks, we can't help but realize this is a decent, well-meaning guy. But it doesn't matter. All Chuck can do is a slow burn.

EXT. SUPERHUB DAY MOMENTS LATER

Distraught, Kelly is helped into the car by Jerry. All those conflicting emotions are roiling through her: the joy that Chuck's alive, the guilt that she's married, the regret, the confused loyalties, everything. It's almost more than one person should ever have to figure out. She starts to get out, to come back, but then she finally gets in. Jerry closes the door and heads around to the driver's side.

INT. READY ROOM SAME

Chuck stands at the window, watching Kelly get back into the car.

INT. PEABODY HOTEL MEMPHIS

We begin on a huge buffet. Great food, including lots of seafood. Bottles of wine and champagne. It's the celebration for Chuck. His welcome-home party. We hear Stan trying to shoo people out and then we WIDEN to reveal we're in the presidential suite, along with Becca, Maynard, various executives we've seen before, and their spouses. Stan's had just a little too much to drink.

                              STAN
      Time to go, people. Time to go. Chuck's had a big day.

                             BECCA
      We do love you, Chuck. We do.

Chuck nods. Thanks.

                            MAYNARD
      I just need to brief him on the meetings tomorrow. The lawyers.
      The accountants.

                              STAN
      It'll keep, it'll keep. Good-night, good-night.

Almost everyone's gone now. Stan turns to Chuck.

                                        STAN (cont'd)
      You got everything you need?

Chuck nods. Sure.

                                        STAN (cont'd)
      Anything you want, anything, you just sign for it. And get some
      sleep. Big day tomorrow. You're not going to believe all the
      paperwork it takes to bring you back. Gotta bring you back to
      life!

He gives Chuck a big hug. A big, warm, half-drunk, full-of-emotion
hug.

                                        STAN (cont'd)
      Gonna bring you back to life!!

The door closes. Chuck is alone. He wanders over to the buffet table.
He picks up a plate of sushi. Raw fish. Forget it. Then he picks up a
crab claw resting in a huge mound of ice. He stares at it. No way he'll
never eat crab again.
He sets it down. His attention is drawn to the sterno cans under the
chafing dishes. The TV plays in the b.g. with the report on Chuck's
welcoming home.

ON TV WELCOMING CEREMONY
On TV, Chuck nods self-consciously, acknowledging the applause of
the crowd, as we saw earlier.

FIRST ANCHOR
That was Chuck Noland today. Home at last. But four years ago,
there was a different ceremony at the Superhub. And Chuck Noland
couldn't be there. We'll leave you with that unforgettable moment.

ON TV-SUPERHUB-MEMORIAL SERVICE-FOUR YEARS EARLIER
We see Fred Smith speaking at a different, more somber ceremony.
He's pointing at a picture of Albert Miller on an easel surrounded by

flowers. He's already been to three other easels. There's one more to go.

                                 FRED SMITH
      Albert Miller.
(he moves on the last photograph)
      Charles "Chuck" Noland.
(beat)
      Five of our finest. We will never forget them.
(beat)
      In their memory, we're going to have a moment of silence. And
      we're going to do something we've never done. We're going to
      stop the line.
(beat)
      Stop the line.

ON TV SUPERHUB
Belts crunch to a stop. Trucks cut their engines. Workers stop in their
tracks. The vast river of packages halts. We see tears on faces.

INT. PEABODY HOTEL SAME
Chuck stares at the images of the line halting, but his hand is on the
sterno can handle.
He turns the handle. The fire goes out. He turns it again. It goes on.
Off. On. Fire. Just like that. He stares at the fire. Impossible for him
to take for granted. We hear the TV.

                          SECOND ANCHOR (ON TV)
      That's an amazing story, Jessica.

                           FIRST ANCHOR (ON TV)
      Can you imagine, Frank, on an island for four years, by your-
      self?

                          SECOND ANCHOR (ON TV)
      Four years in the South Pacific, Jessica? Sounds great to me.

But it's a happy ending, Frank. Chuck Noland is home. And he'll never have to be alone again.

And there Chuck is. Very much alone. Again. He turns the fire off.

SECOND ANCHOR (ON TV)

In other news, the Tennessee Titans cut wide receiver Omar Jones –

INT. PEABODY HOTEL LATER THAT NIGHT

It's dead quiet, except for the occasional jarring urban sound: traffic, a siren. A roll of thunder. A light switches on. And off. We PAN past the bed. The coverlet, pillows and top sheet have been stripped off it. We go past them. There, on the floor, is Chuck.

The light switches on. Then off. On. Then off. Chuck has the cord switch for the lamp in one hand, the watch with Kelly's picture in the other. The light comes on. We see Kelly's face. The light goes off. She's gone. On, here. Off, gone. It's the same way he looked at her picture on the island.

EXT. KELLY HOUSE LATER THAT NIGHT

It's raining. A taxi pulls up to a darkened house in Chickasaw Gardens. A few kid toys and a baby swing are in the side yard.

INT. TAXI SAME

The DRIVER turns to Chuck.

DRIVER

How long you gonna be?

He doesn't have a clue. He pulls out a twenty from a packet of cash.

CHUCK

How long does this buy me?

DRIVER

Twenty minutes.

CHUCK

If I'm not out by then, you go on. I'll call when I need a ride.

DRIVER

It's raining pigs and chickens out there. You wanta borrow my jacket?

Rain? Who cares about rain?

CHUCK

No thanks. I don't need it.

And he opens the door.

EXT. TAXI SAME

Chuck walks toward the front porch, ignoring the rain.

EXT. KELLY HOUSE NIGHT MOMENTS LATER

Chuck reaches the porch, sheltered from the rain. Now the impulse and determination that brought him here give way to practicality. What to do? His hand goes to the bell, goes down. Goes again. Suddenly the door opens. It's Kelly. She's in a tee-shirt and shorts. Her eyes are red as if she's been crying.

KELLY

I'm awake. I saw your taxi drive up.

For the longest moment they stare at each other. All that emotion, all the anticipation, is down to this, standing on the front porch in the rain. And it's okay. They're doing it.

KELLY (cont'd)

Get out of the rain, for God's sake.

And she ushers him inside.

INT. KELLY HOUSE CONTINUOUS

She brings him inside, then comes into his arms. For a moment they hold each other, a feeling they both had thought would never happen again.

> KELLY
>
> You're so thin.

> CHUCK
>
> You smell so good.

But that's a little too intimate so she breaks away.

> KELLY
>
> Come on. I'll make you some coffee.

She leads him toward the kitchen. Chuck looks upstairs. Jerry? The baby?

> KELLY (cont'd)
> (whispers)
> Sleeping.

INT. KELLY HOUSE NIGHT CONTINUOUS

She leads him to the kitchen through a sort of all-purpose family room filled with kid's toys and family memorabilia. Chuck takes it all in. Every object speaks volumes to the life he didn't get to have.

> CHUCK
>
> Nice house.

> KELLY
>
> Yeah, we've got a nice mortgage too.

As she busies herself reheating the coffee he holds out the watch.

CHUCK

I brought you this.

(beat)

It's broken.

(beat)

I kept the picture. It's all faded.

KELLY

I can't believe you saved that old thing.

(beat)

You should keep it. I gave it to you.

CHUCK

It's a family watch. It belongs in your family.

She takes it reluctantly. Her family's not Chuck's family any more. She opens the refrigerator. On the door are magnets holding family snapshots, to-do lists, kids' drawings… and a calendar with a big photograph of Kelly, Jerry, and their daughter.

CHUCK (cont'd)

Your little girl – she's beautiful.

Kelly looks at the photo.

KELLY

She's a handful.

CHUCK

What's her name?

KELLY

Katie.

There's no safe ground, what to talk about?

CHUCK

There's one thing I want to get straight.

Terrified, she looks up at him.

CHUCK (cont'd)

Who are the Titans? Do we have a football team now?

KELLY

(relieved)

Yeah. They used to be in Houston. First they were the Oilers, then the Titans.

CHUCK

The Houston Oilers? Are in Tennessee?

KELLY

That's not all. They went to the Super Bowl last year.

CHUCK

They went to the Super Bowl. And I missed it?

For a moment the old easiness between them comes back.

KELLY

You would have died! It was so exciting! They almost won. By one yard! One lousy yard, that's all it was, right at the end.

CHUCK

But I don't get it. Why aren't they here? In Memphis?

KELLY

Oh, God, don't even ask. Just the thought of it sends Fred Smith into orbit.

CHUCK

The good news, Fred, is that Tennessee's finally getting an NFL team. The bad news is, it's in Nashville.

She laughs. He does too. She hands him the coffee.

> KELLY
> We've got whole milk, two per cent, non fat. But no half and half. I know how much you love it.

> CHUCK
> That's okay. I'm not so picky anymore.

He takes a sip of coffee. So good.

> CHUCK (cont'd)
> So, are you a professor now? Dr. Kelly?

> KELLY
> Oh, that. I gave all that up.

There's a long silence.

> KELLY (cont'd)
> But I'm thinking of taking it up again.

But that's awkward, too. Every subject seems to be a minefield. As they talk, Chuck notices the big dining table which is covered with maps, magazines, and newspapers, some new, some starting to fade a little. Chuck picks up some of the older papers.

> KELLY (cont'd)
> It's everything. From when you went down, to now. There's your obituary. Not many people get to read that.

As he picks up the obituary, she looks through the maps.

> KELLY (cont'd)
> They never figured out what caused that crash. Probably some

hazardous material caught fire...

She pulls out a big map of the Pacific covered with hand-drawn circles and grids.

> KELLY (cont'd)
> Look. Here's where that ship found you. You'd drifted 500 miles. Right here, you must have just missed the shipping lanes.

Chuck looks at the vast expanse of blue. Kelly points to another circle she's drawn in the middle of the ocean.

> KELLY (cont'd)
> That's where your island was... about 600 miles south of the Cook Islands.

She points to some grids that don't quite touch the circle.

> KELLY (cont'd)
> And these were the search grids. They went back and forth for weeks looking for you.

Chuck stares at the map.

> CHUCK
> They were really close.

> KELLY
> Yeah, they were.

> CHUCK
> I never should have got on that plane. I never should have got out of the car.

She stares at him, not knowing what to say. Then she gets an idea that makes her smile.

KELLY

Come on. I want to show you something.

EXT. GARAGE NIGHT

RRRRRRRR. The garage door cranks open, revealing Chuck's old Jeep Cherokee and a Camry.

CHUCK

You kept the car?

KELLY

I kept everything.

Chuck runs his hand along the side of the car.

CHUCK

Could I, could I take this out?

KELLY

Chuck, it's your car. You can have it.

She hands him the key chain, which still has the Swiss Army knife on it. Chuck regards the knife for a moment.

CHUCK

This would have come in handy.

She opens the back door.

KELLY

Just got to clean a few things out.
(beat)
Could you give me a hand?

He opens the other back door. There's a BABY SEAT in the middle of the back seat. Together they struggle to release the seat belt, then Kelly passes it over to Chuck.

CHUCK

Are you going to have more kids?

KELLY

Just feed it though there. No... through that doohickey there.
(now answering his question)
I don't know. It's kind of confusing right now.

Chuck finally gets the belt released.

CHUCK

You should. You really should. I would.

Kelly pulls out the baby seat, revealing half-eaten teething biscuits, a
toy, a tiny book.
For a moment her eyes meet Chuck's. This is really what he missed.
And Kelly knows it and feels it.

KELLY

So. What now?

CHUCK

I don't know.
(beat)
I really don't know.

Chuck gets into the driver's seat. Kelly stands by the door, leaning
down on it, watching him, really close now.
He turns the key and starts the engine. She's staring at him, all the
emotion bubbling up. His hand goes to her face, his eyes saying, you
are so beautiful.

KELLY

Right back, you said you'd be right back.

CHUCK

I'm so sorry.

KELLY

Me too.

They have a sweet kiss through the window, safe with the car door
between them. Then it has to be over and it is. He looks at her with
as much of a smile as he can muster. Then he puts the car in reverse
and backs out into the rain.
We stay with Kelly as it backs out and onto the road. Then it stops,
goes in gear and starts to move forward – slowly, as if Chuck can't
quite bear to leave.
But she can't stand it. She runs after him, into the rain.

KELLY (cont'd)

Chuck!!!

EXT. KELLY HOUSE SAME

Kelly runs down the driveway, but the Jeep is gone. Suddenly it backs
into frame! Chuck jumps out and runs toward her through the rain.
She comes into his arms. They're both soaked. She kisses him totally
and utterly, and he her back. Chuck holds her tight. God, how he
dreamed of this. For the longest time we watch them embrace in the
rain, water pouring off them.
Then he helps her into the car.

INT. CHUCK'S CAR SAME

She's breathing hard, her hair soaked, tears and rain on her face. She
tries to explain, her breath coming in gasps.

KELLY

I always knew you were alive. I knew it. But they said I had to
stop saying that. I had to give you up. So I tried. Jerry was
there for me. He's so good. A good father. I love him.

(beat)

But I've always loved you. You're the love of my life.

(beat)

Oh God, I don't know what to do.

Now it's up to Chuck.

                    CHUCK
I love you, Kelly.
(beat)
    More than you'll ever know.

Chuck starts the car.

                    KELLY
Chuck...

He looks at her for a long time. This is the moment. Forward,
together. Or back, to her house. With him. Or with them.

                    CHUCK
    You have to go home.

He puts the car in gear. And pulls into the driveway.

EXT. KELLY HOUSE NIGHT CONTINUOUS
And the car drives back toward Kelly's house. It reaches the garage
and stops. For the longest moment we watch it sit there, in the rain.
Then the passenger door opens and Kelly gets out. Kelly stands
watching in the rain as Chuck pulls out and drives down the street.
Good-bye.

INT. STAN'S HOUSE LATER THAT NIGHT
It's still raining. Stan and Chuck sit in Stan's den: a TV, a couple of
LaZyBoys, a bookcase with a few books, some FedEx mementos,
some pictures of Stan and his late wife Mary. They've both put a
good dent in a bottle of Jack Daniels. Chuck has a towel draped over
his wet shirt.

                    CHUCK
    We both did the math. Kelly added it all up and had to let me
    go. Me, I was never getting off that island. I was going to get
    sick, injured, I was going to die there. Totally alone. The only

choice I had – the only thing I could still control – was when and how I would die.

It's all coming back to him, carrying the rope up to the summit.

> CHUCK (cont'd)
> So I made a rope and went up to hang myself. But I had to test it first – you know me. The log broke the tree limb! I couldn't even kill myself the way I wanted to. I had power over NOTH-ING. And that's when this feeling came over me – like a warm blanket. And I knew, not up here –

He means, not in his brain.

> CHUCK (cont'd)
> – but in some deep part of me – I just knew – I had to stay alive. Even if I had no reason to hope. Even if my logic told me I'd never see any of this again.

"This" being the whole world he knew.

> CHUCK (cont'd)
> And that's what I did, just kept breathing.

He remembers the way he was when we saw him eating the fish, those dead eyes.

> CHUCK (cont'd)
> That's all I did. Just stayed alive. And you know what? The sun came up, and the sun went down, and all my logic was wrong. Because the tide brought me – a sail.

He means, a miracle, and even low as he is he has to smile at the form that sail took.

> CHUCK (cont'd)
> And now here I am, back in Memphis, sitting with you. And

145

there's ice in my glass.

His eyes are moist now. He and Stan share a long look.

> CHUCK (cont'd)
> And I've lost her all over again and it hurts. So damn much.
> You know.

Stan does know. He's been there.

> CHUCK (cont'd)
> But I'm grateful, I am so grateful, she was with me on that
> island. And I know what I've got to do, no matter how bad it
> gets. I've got to keep breathing. Just keep breathing.

There's a sense of hope here, a hard-won knowledge at the core of
life.

> CHUCK (cont'd)
> Because tomorrow – the sun is going to rise, and who knows
> what the tide could bring?

EXT. TEXAS WIDE
Boom!! Rainy night gives way to the shock of a great expanse of
Texas blue sky.

INT. CHUCK'S JEEP CHEROKEE DAY SAME
Guzzling water out of a bottle, Chuck drives, staring out at the vast
expanse of space stretching horizon to horizon, just as he had stared
at the ocean. In the great American tradition, he's hit the road to
purge his emotions. And to do something else. He's got one last package to deliver.

EXT. MOBEETIE, TEXAS DAY WIDE
Chuck's Jeep Cherokee heads down a ranch road and comes to a
four-cornered intersection.

EXT. MOBEETIE, TEXAS/INT. CHUCK'S CAR DAY

Chuck stops the car and sips from a big Dairy Queen drink. The Angel Wing Box is on the seat beside him, along with a new Wilson volleyball and a sheaf of printed directions. Chuck checks the directions, trying to figure out where to go. Okay. Go to the right. He makes the turn.

EXT. MOBEETIE, TEXAS DAY

He drives up to the artist studio/residence we saw in the very beginning and gets out of the car. On the way to the door he passes the mailbox. The iron script on top once read "Dick and Bettina Peterson." The "Dick" has been burned off with a welding torch. Dick's history. Chuck takes a moment to consider the sculptures in the yard.

EXT. MOBEETIE, TEXAS DAY

Chuck's been knocking at the door for a while. One last time.

                              CHUCK
     Anybody??

Nothing. He heads back to the car.

EXT. MOBEETIE, TEXAS DAY CAR

Chuck scribbles a note on one of the printed map pages. "This package saved my life." Writes his name and phone number.

EXT. MOBEETIE, TEXAS DAY MOMENTS LATER

He leaves the faded Angel Wing Box in the door and wedges the note behind it.

EXT. MOBEETIE, TEXAS DAY WIDE

His car drives away from the house.

EXT. MOBEETIE, TEXAS DAY MOMENTS LATER

Chuck's car is stopped at the four corners. Chuck has the map spread out on the hood of the car, trying to figure out where to go. A pickup truck drives past. Stops. Backs up. There's a WOMAN inside. An interesting, off-beat, confident woman with a twinkle in her eye.

WOMAN

You look lost.

CHUCK

I do?

She gets out and heads over to check the map on the hood.

WOMAN

Where are you headed?

CHUCK

I was just about to figure that out.

WOMAN

Okay, straight ahead, that'll hook you to 83 South, Childress, Abilene, down to Mexico. Left, that goes to the 40 East. Memphis, Nashville, the Atlantic. Right, that's Amarillo, Flagstaff –

CHUCK

The Pacific.

WOMAN

Back that way, there's a whole lot of nothing, all the way to Canada.
(beat)
You sure you're okay?

He smiles as he thinks of all the possibilities.

CHUCK

I'm great.

148

And he looks it. She smiles at him, an open, West Texas smile.

                                    WOMAN
          Then good luck, Cowboy.

                                    CHUCK
          Thank you.
Just as the first word he uttered – "Time" – defined who he was at
the beginning, so these last words – "Thank you" – give us some idea
of the humility and gratitude he has now. The woman gets back in
her pickup and heads down the road Chuck just drove up. On the tail
gate of her truck is painted… a set of ANGEL WINGS. Chuck stares at
them. That must be… that must be the woman who drew the Wings!!
His guardian Angel Wings!!

EXT. MOBEETIE, TEXAS DAY CLOSE ON CHUCK
After a long moment Chuck begins to smile – a wise, hard-earned
smile. It doesn't really matter which way he goes. At some point in
life's grand journey you just have to let go of the oars and have faith.
His new life begins… now. The end is the beginning.

FADE OUT.

Cast In Order of Appearance

Ramon PAUL SANCHEZ
Bettina Peterson LARI WHITE
Fyodor LEONID CITER
Dick Peterson DAVID ALLEN BROOKS
Beautiful Russian Woman YELENA PAPOVIC
Russian Babushka VALENTINA ANANYINA
Nicolai SEMION SUDARIKOV
Chuck Noland TOM HANKS
Yuri PETER VON BERG
Lev DMITRI S. BOUDRINE
French FedEx Loader FRANÇOIS DUHAMEL
Pilot Jack MICHAEL FOREST
Pilot Gwen VIVEKA DAVIS
Stan NICK SEARCY
Memphis State Student JENNIFER CHOE
Kelly Frears HELEN HUNT
Kelly's Mother NAN MARTIN
Anne Larson ANNE BELLAMY
Dennis Larson DENNIS LETTS
Wendy Larson WENDY WORTHINGTON
Skye Larson SKYE McKENZIE
Virginia Larson VALERIE WILDMAN
John Larson JOHN DUERLER
Steve Larson STEVE MONROE
Lindsey Larson ASHLEY & LINDSEY TREFGER
Katie Larson ALYSSA, KAITLYN & LAUREN GAINER
Gregory Larson ALBERT & GREGORY PUGLIESE
Matt Larson BRANDON & MATTHEW REINHART
Lisa Madden LISA LONG
Lauren Madden LAUREN BIRKELL

Elden Madden ELDEN HENSON
Morgan Stockton TIMOTHY STACK
Alice Stockton ALICE VAUGHN
Chase Stockton CHASE BEBAK
Gage Stockton GAGE BEBAK
Amanda Stockton AMANDA & ANDREA CAGNEY
Fred Stockton FRED & PETER SEMMER
Joe Wally JOE CONLEY
Ralph Wally AARON RAPKE
Pilot Al VIN MARTIN
Pilot Blaine GARRET DAVIS
Pilot Peter JAY ACOVONE
Pilot Kevin CHRISTOPHER KRIESA
Jerry Lovett CHRIS NOTH
Fred Smith AS HIMSELF
FedEx Anchor #1 MICHELLE ROBINSON
FedEx Anchor #2 TOMMY CRESSWELL
Becca Twig JENIFER LEWIS
Maynard Graham GEOFFREY BLAKE
FedEx Manager RICH SICKLER
Taxi Driver DERICK ALEXANDER

William Broyles, Jr., (Screenwriter) a decorated marine veteran, received an Academy Award® nomination and Writer's Guild Award nomination for *Apollo 13*, which he co-wrote with longtime friend and colleague Al Reinert. Their screenplay won the PEN Center Literary Award for best screenplay. Broyles wrote Tim Burton's reinvention of *Planet of the Apes*, which Twentieth Century Fox will release in Summer 2001. In 1999 he wrote *Entrapment*, starring Sean Connery and Catherine Zeta-Jones.

Broyles was founding editor of the award-winning Texas Monthly magazine, editor-in-chief for California magazine, and editor-in-chief of Newsweek. He has written for numerous magazines, authored the book *Brothers in Arms*, and was the co-creator of the television series *China Beach*, which won 12 Emmys®. He currently is working on several books and screenplays.

Robert Zemeckis (Director/Producer) earned the Best Director Oscar® for *Forrest Gump*, which also was named Best Picture and earned Tom Hanks the Best Actor Oscar® in 1995. In 2000, Zemeckis produced and directed the psychological thriller *What Lies Beneath*, starring Harrison Ford and Michelle Pfeiffer. Both *Cast Away* and *What Lies Beneath* are the premiere film projects for ImageMovers, the production company Zemeckis established in 1998 with partners Steve Starkey and Jack Rapke.

His other films include *Contact*, starring Jodie Foster and based on the best-selling novel by Carl Sagan, and the box-office smash *Who Framed Roger Rabbit*, which became the top-grossing film of 1988. In 1985 he directed and co-wrote *Back to the Future*, which also topped the annual box-office chart. Zemeckis went on to direct the film's two sequels, completing one the most popular film trilogies ever. His other films include *Romancing the Stone*, *Death Becomes Her*, *Used Cars*, and I *Wanna Hold Your Hand*.

Tom Hanks (Actor, Producer) starred as Chuck Noland in *Cast Away*, as well as serving as a producer on the film. In 1999, Hanks starred in the Oscar®-nominated drama *The Green Mile*.

That same year saw Hanks receive the Golden Globe Award and his fourth Academy Award® nomination for his role as Captain Miller in Steven Spielberg's *Saving Private Ryan*. Hanks received widespread critical and audience acclaim for his work in *Apollo 13*, in which he starred as astronaut Jim Lovell. In 1995, he became the first actor in more than fifty years to win back-to-back Best Actor Academy Awards® when he took home his second Oscar® for an unforgettable performance in the title role of Robert Zemeckis's *Forrest Gump*. His work in the film also brought him a Golden Globe Award and a Screen Actors Guild Award. The year before, he had been honored with his first Academy Award®, as well as a Golden Globe Award for Best Actor, for his moving portrayal of AIDS-stricken lawyer Andrew Beckett in Jonathan Demme's *Philadelphia*.